Sucker PUNCHED!™

How to Rise to the Top After Being Punched Down

Sucker PUNCHED!™

How to Rise
to the Top
After Being
Punched Down

Dr. Gayle Joplin Hall

Dedication

I dedicate this book
to my mother, Lonva Hall,
and to my father, Dwain Hall.

♥♥

I am so blessed to be born unto you.
You both have shown me unconditional love
and have taught me the importance of family.
You instilled in me the value system I have today.
I am forever grateful for the love you bring into my life.

Foreword

Sucker Punched!™ *is a no holds barred resource for achieving a high level of happiness in life in spite of the slug fests and emotional punches that we sometimes experience during our earthly sojourn.*

Dr. Gayle Joplin Hall's stories will tug at your heart strings and cause tears to well up in your eyes. You will feel deep sorrow for the slugs you or others have taken and then...she turns it all around makes your heart soar to wonderful emotional heights with simple, easy to understand and apply solutions!

With this book you will learn ways to think, feel and do things differently so you can dodge or avoid sucker punches and come out the winner in all of the battles of life! Dr. Hall shows you super simple ways that will cause you to function at the highest levels. She tells you clearly HOW to deal with negative blows that life and people throw at you.

If your life has been tough and full of unpleasant experiences, bad parenting, bullies, mean peers or hurtful relationships, this book is for you. Be prepared to learn at deep and profound levels!

> ~ Jack M. Zufelt, Author of the #1 best selling
> book, *The DNA of Success*
> International Keynote Speaker and Trainer.
>
> www.dnaofsuccess.com
> www.jackzufeltspeaks.com

Advance Praise and Testimonials

~ *Right away, the title* **Sucker Punched!**™ *captured my attention. I couldn't believe someone actually wrote about being sucker punched. I could relate to Dr. Hall's book on so many levels that it was scary. Gayle not only described a sucker punch, but took it to multiple levels and situations as to how a person can be sucker punched. The book also asked some very thought provoking questions at the end of every chapter. The questions made me dig deep in to my soul and face the hard truths I was too afraid to ask myself. Then, just when I wondered if there was ever a way to deal with a sucker punch, she outlined exactly what I needed to do and how I could handle different sucker punches. I loved that she shared her personal experiences with being sucker punched. It made me feel like I wasn't all alone. I have known Gayle for 18 years and she managed to hide many of these embarrassing secrets from me. We were very good friends, too! I highly recommend* **Sucker Punched!**™ *by Dr. Gayle Hall to anyone and everyone who's ever experienced such deep pain. This book will make you laugh and cry and deal with reality like no other book out there!*

> Anneliese Smith, Health and Wellness Fitness
> Educator at Blue Cross and Blue Shield of Montana

~ *Dr. Hall's book,* **Sucker Punched!**™, *offers remarkably refreshing insights into oft-tread turf. With deeply felt honesty, warmth, sharp expertise and a wide-sweeping breadth of knowledge, you know you've discovered something groundbreaking and emotionally rewarding within the first few pages of this book!*

I love that Dr. Hall is willing to take on the tough topics; her writing is brave, engaging, and absolutely compelling. There is advice, counsel, exploration of issues that plague post-modern relationships. What sets this book apart is Dr. Hall's open and outspoken gutsy intelligence and a willingness to push the envelope...a great distance. For real solutions to real-life problems and a much-needed break from the ordinary revisited tone on dealing with surviving and thriving in modern relationships, **Sucker Punched!**™ *will become the go-to sourcebook. Thanks, Dr. Hall, for your willingness to tell the truth, with wisdom and great meaning. This book will have resonance for so many, on so many levels!*

Doug Winters, Author and Musician, *The Musical Stylings of Bob James,* 1981, Warner Bros.

~ *Dr. Gayle Joplin Hall has written a profound book,* **Sucker Punched!**™, *one that most of us can relate to, one where we have at one time or another, walked in those same shoes. She takes you through a visual and emotional journey of personal experiences, the sucker punches that can impact your entire life and cause you to make serious choices that will determine your future. Dr. Hall then provides the lessons we can learn, and constructive steps to take, to turn all of those painful punches into positive, life-transforming decisions. Her candid approach may surprise you at times, but it is in this straightforward and compassionate writing that you, yourself, can be awakened to all the possibilities of taking those sour lemons of life and making them into the best lemonade you ever had!*

Rita Rocker, National Speaker, Author and Coach, Transformation Academy, LLC

~ *Dr. Gayle Hall has created a dynamic blueprint for overcoming adversity and flourishing, regardless of how many sucker punches you have endured. This poignant book,* **Sucker Punched!**™, *is for everyone who has survived childhood throughout adulthood. By following Gayle's system, you will learn how to keep the Sucker Punched Syndrome*™ *(SPS) at bay. You will be able to go from pitiful to powerful.*

Lisa Schilling, RN, Author of *"The Get REAL Guide to Health and Fitness"* Wellness Nurse Strategist
www.getrealwellnesssolutions.com

~ *In the sea of self-help material that permeates the shelves, Dr. Gayle J. Hall's* **Sucker Punched!**™, *stands head and shoulders above the rest. Written in the 'confessional self-help' style, like my own Midlife Metamorphosis, Dr. Hall not only chronicles her own experiences of being sucker punched in life, but has also turned her book into a learning experience by adding contemplative questions at the end of each chapter. This makes* **Sucker Punched!**™ *a very unique and wonderful experience to read and one that you will benefit highly from reading.*

> Jim Rogers, Author of *Midlife Metamorphosis -The Naked Truth About Becoming Your Loving Self*, Midlife Heart Coach, and creator of the *Become Your Loving Self* course.

~ *Dr. Gayle Joplin Hall is a highly inspirational writer, speaker, and Professor. I have rarely encountered an individual so passionately dedicated to the causes she believes in or that of helping the underprivileged. I also learned the values of listening to and learning about people just from knowing Dr. Hall. Encased in this small beautiful frame, with her fabulous smile and joyous laughter, is the heart of a warrior.*

In her own unique way, as only Dr. Gayle Hall could say it, **Sucker Punched!**™, *exposed me to her experiences at the hands of bullies. Tormented first at the age of six years old, she began to feel the vulnerability of being small, and feeling unloved and unprotected.*

Stories such as the ones told in **Sucker Punched!**™ *are lived out daily all over this world. Dr. Hall has lived an extraordinary life. She has survived the ridicule, humiliation, and pain of domestic violence, lost loves, and bullying. She has achieved her dreams despite the negative people around her. Those who tried so hard to hold her down and hold her back will never be her obstacle again. Dr. Hall is a determined and fierce protector of the victims of domestic abuse, social injustice, and those ritually intimidated by bullies.*

> Shawn Elizabeth Blackwelder, Nurse,
> JPS Hospital, Ft. Worth, TX

~ Dr. Hall has written a highly personal, yet theoretically sound narrative that offers a readily-applied approach to help those who have been bullied overcome their past and take power over their future. Yes, it really does balance personal testimony, theoretical understanding and practical solutions! **Sucker Punched!**™, should be a standard tool for victims and those who work with victims, helping them to move forward as victors. This book will also be helpful to those who, though they may not see themselves as victims, are trying to become smarter and stronger because of adversities they have faced. This book is a significant contribution to the literature on resiliency, self-empowerment and self-agency.

> M. Frank Stluka, Sociologist, educator, author, youth devel-opment specialist, and workforce development professional

~ I read your book, **Sucker Punched!**™, Dr. Gayle Hall, and I absolutely LOVE it. Everything about it resonates with me, from the title of the book to the chapters and content. This is a "must-read" book because everyone can relate to this. Why? Because everyone in their life has been sucker punched. Not once, but many, many times. Reading this book will make them stronger individuals. By the way, being sucker punched in the love department is the one in which I feel most people will relate with. Since there are so many people that have gone through a divorce, are unsuccessful at finding the 'right partner,' etc., I really related to that chapter, personally. Dr. Hall has added questions at the end of each chapter to help you really think through ways in your own life of how to handle situations. If you don't run out and buy a copy of this book for yourself and several for your friends, you will end up being sucker punched over and over again.

> Dennisse Mixter, Entrepreneur, Miami, FL

~ **Sucker Punched!**™ is an inspiring book. Dr. Hall's personal story is empowering and is written so that anyone who reads this book can iden-tify with it. Artfully inserted references, journaling suggestions, and easy to *understand explanations of highly relevant psychological theories and concepts makes this a real tool for recovery and self transformation.*

Alma Castaneda, LPCS
Owner at Alma Castaneda, LPCS.

~ *I have felt like I've been sucker punched all of my life. It's been one thing after another. When I was a kid, I was constantly picked on. Everyone liked my sisters, but no one liked me. Before I got a divorce, I felt really sucker punched when I read an entry in my ex-husband's facebook, he found his soul mate, but it was not me. Time and time again, I got sucker punched. I kept asking myself, "what's wrong with me?" When I read* **Sucker Punched!**™, *I couldn't put the book down. I realized that I'm not the only one... I'm not the only person who has been sucker punched time and time again. I'm normal—it's not me! I had to see what happened next and how Dr. Gayle Hall dealt with the pain. I have many issues I am dealing with now. I had to see if there was anything that could "fix" me. With the help of this witty, but serious workbook, I am on the road to understanding how to avoid being sucker punched ever again. Thank goodness for* **Sucker Punched!**™

Pam Pritchard, Customer Service Analyst II for a Long Term Care Insurance Company

Acknowledgments

There are a few specific people who I must name because without them, this book would have never come to fruition. First and foremost, I must thank "J". "J" has been steadfast and resolute throughout this journey. On the days I could not get the words to flow and could not get into my "zone," "J" fed me, comforted me, and understood that I had writer's block. "J" saw the tears flow as I re-lived some of my most painful memories while I was writing Sucker Punched!™ and all the while, understood this was a catharsis for me. Never once, did "J" leave my side.

Additionally, I would like to thank my best friend who has endured my trials and tribulations for the past 20 years. Tracy has been by my side, even though we are 500 miles apart. Her devoted love has helped me more than she will ever realize. Other friends have helped to hold my hand all the way through this journey as well. You know who you are.

To my family members, especially my parents, oldest brother, sister, and my youngest son, I love you more than life itself. Thank you for the encouraging words and for believing in me.

I also must thank my Publisher, Michelle Prince and Project Manager, Cheryl Callighan. Cheryl's patience is akin to that of a saint. I made many changes in order to have my book cover "be just perfect" and Cheryl was most willing to facilitate my wishes.

Thank you to the children and teens who felt safe enough with me to be able to share their stories of bullying and abuse. This is a widespread phenomenon and must be brought to a standstill. To the women and men who filled out self-report data and questionnaires at homeless shelters, safe houses, in college class rooms, on the street, and face-to-face, thank you for your courage. You have helped those who have not walked in your shoes to understand what it feels like to hit rock-bottom, lose sense of self-identity, self-worth, and endure feelings of worthlessness. You are so determined to rise back to the top again. I know you will make it.

The next few books are anthologies of Sucker Punched!™. The books will have stories from those who are homeless, who have been victims of domestic violence, have lost their jobs, been duped, suffered a mid-life crisis, or have been involved in a sucker punched relationship, as mentioned above. If you would like to tell your story, please contact me for one of my upcoming books.

Finally, to those reading this book who are still stuck in circumstances beyond your control that are dragging you down and leaving you feeling sucker punched, please make a plan. Start off with small, doable goals, perhaps even daily goals, then set weekly goals, and move on to bigger long-term goals. Let that warrior spirit shine through. You CAN do this!

Table of Contents

For more information about the author, Dr. Gayle Joplin Hall, please visit her website: www.DrHallonCall.com *Be sure to sign up on the email list and become part of our community. We are growing and do not want to leave you behind.

GODSPEED, BE HAPPY, AND LIVE YOUR BEST LIFE NOW!

Dr. Gayle Joplin Hall

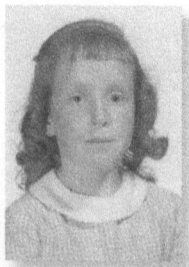

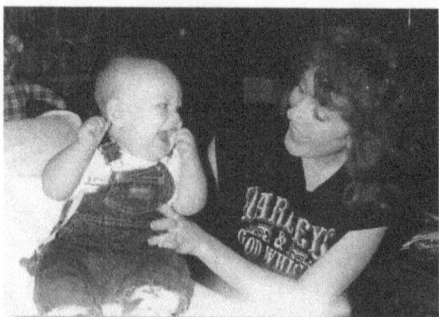

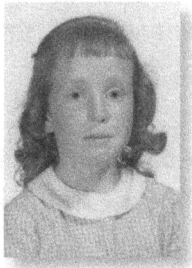

CHAPTER

What "Sucker Punched" Means and How it Feels to be Sucker Punched

"Ever since I was a little kid, I was afraid of being hit in the belly. Perhaps that came from being bullied my entire life, until I was fifteen years old. It wasn't easy to be the smallest one in my class and to stick out like a sore thumb with freckles and red hair. I always felt out of place. I was teased, called names, and I cried almost daily until I grew to be smart and cute during my sophomore year in high school. That shut the bullies up. And those lessons as a child? Well, they prepared me for what was to come as an adult. I was sucker punched as an adult, over and over again."

~ Dr. Gayle Joplin Hall.

The Definition of "Sucker Punched"

Merriam Webster's Online Dictionary provides a super simple explanation of sucker punched. It's defined exactly like this: "This is a transitive verb meaning, 'To punch a person suddenly without warning and often without apparent provocation.' " The title of this book is *"Sucker Punched!"*™ in the past tense, because all of the examples are from my past life experiences. If you, too, were sucker punched, you most likely will be able to relate to several of these examples yourself, from your own prior experiences. And my guess is that it did not feel good to you, either!

Let's Begin By Saying the Dirty Little Word, "Sucker Punched"

What do you instantly think of when you hear the sentence, "She's been sucker punched again!" Do you think of a loser, someone who just doesn't have her act together, a person who deserves "bad luck" or someone who likes to be on the pity-party chair? Honestly, what immediately comes to your mind when you hear the words, "sucker punched"?

Do you see a dried-up, little, old, drunken man begging on the street corner, using filthy language and swearing like a sailor? Do you think of a woman who is a drug addict—one who may prefer her meth addiction to feeding and taking care of her children for the week? Or do you see families who are on welfare, at the homeless shelter, or living on the street and assume they're lazy and thus deserve their present situation? What if I were to tell you that anyone can be sucker punched, regardless of his or her socioeconomic status? Would you believe me?

2

Psychologists' Theories Are Still Being Challenged Today

Almost every psychologist since the early 1900's, has stated how important the infant, preschool, and adolescent years of development are in one's mental well-being. Erik Erikson's Psychosocial Developmental Theory is one of the most widely known because he states that we never stop learning, growing, and developing throughout our entire lifetime. Erikson's theory is based on the premise that we must master specific tasks in each of the eight stages of life before moving on to the next stage of life. If the tasks in a stage aren't fulfilled, a negative consequence will make the next stage of life more difficult to deal with. Children and adults who continue to move though phases of life without mastering the stages and specific tasks in life, will face difficulties and frustration while trying to mature and make headway as a person.

The Early Years of Development, Bullying, and Hand-Made Dresses

When we are babies and in pre-school, we're protected by our parents and learn from them, just as we learn from our environment and those around us. If at an early age, we are detached for any length of time from our parents or protectors, we may become vulnerable to bullies and labeled as "sissies." Once labeled, this message may carry over throughout adolescence. The same is true for learning disabled children, any children with handicaps or special needs, or children who are "different" for any reason.

Perhaps the basis is for pure socioeconomic reasons. Suppose your parents weren't as wealthy as the rest of the people in the neighborhood. Maybe you were of a minority status or were an outcast because of being stereotyped for any reason at an early age. Were you a different color than other kids in your neighborhood? Were you the only kid in school with red hair or kinky, curly hair? Did your parents drive a different car, or not even have a car? Did you wear clothes that were "home-made" instead of purchased from stores? I was "sucker punched" for wearing clothes that my mother sewed for me until I was thirteen years old. Now, I would give anything to have my mother be able to sew for me once again.

Chickens and a Rooster

When I was living on a farm with my Grandmother in rural Kansas one winter, I missed my mother and daddy so much. Almost every night, I had the chore of "putting the chickens in the pen," which was not easy for me to do. I was tiny—I stood only forty-two and a half inches tall and weighed only thirty-four pounds. My older brother was taller than I was, yet he never had to go out in the dark to put those chickens away. I'd get all bundled up in my boots and coat, carry the lantern, reach for the hook on the top of the fence post and try to wrestle all the chickens into the coop. In addition to the darkness and the desolate, howling winds, quite often, a huge rooster loved to chase me. I was terrified of that rooster.

The first time my Grandma Hall taught me to "put the chickens away" she told me this would be my nightly chore while staying with them. As she was demonstrating the proper way to open the gate and close it so the chickens couldn't escape, the rooster approached us and she yelled at him to get away. Instead of leaving, he prepared to attack her. She grabbed a stick and poked him with it saying, "This is why you're now doing this job, Gayle. The rooster doesn't like me. He will like you.

4

But, be careful, because if he catches you, he will peck your eyes out." It struck me motionless with fear. Every night after dinner, I had to put those chickens away and be chased by a rooster that, I felt, was half as big as me. No wonder I had nightmares until my mid-twenties.

Getting That First Blow—Who Would Dream a Six-Year-Old Could be Sucker Punched?

That was the first major blow for me, a massive sucker punch when I was only six years old. My parents had decided that my older brother and I should live for six months with my paternal grandparents in rural Kansas while they, along with my two younger siblings, lived with my father's brother in Kansas City. My parents had four little kids under the age of seven to care for. They had to find a home to purchase in the Kansas City area. My father needed to secure employment after he'd left the Navy and life in San Diego, when my parents made the decision to move back to the Midwest.

I don't know when my grandmother began disliking me—whether it was the first time she ever saw me or when she had to care for me daily during this period in my family's life. She disliked me immensely. Actually, she hated me. Daily, my grandmother compared me to my mother in a negative fashion (my paternal grandmother disliked my mother very much). Of course, she would never say anything to my mother's face, just to mine. Can you imagine how this might affect a young child's psyche and self esteem to hear bad comments over and over about her own mother and how her mother "did not want her"? Every day, my grandmother told me that my mother did not want me and that was why I had to stay with them on the farm. I heard this repeatedly.

5

The hugs, kisses, and love that a six-year-old needs from her grandmother were absent, so I felt very abandoned. My parents visited every two weeks; nonetheless, I felt deserted by my parents and unloved by my grandmother. I begged and pleaded with my parents to take me back with them. I cried and tried to explain how awful it was for me at Grandma's house, but my entreaties went unheard. I know my parents were doing the best they could do. As young parents with four little kids, they had no other options. They never understood how much one person, my father's own mother, could hate one little red headed kid—me.

Erikson's Theory of Psychosocial Development states that during this period of life, a child should be motivated to accomplish tasks and solve problems, while receiving much encouragement from parents and others. But to my grandmother, nothing I did was good enough. My older brother was the favored one and could do no wrong. Every day, my grandmother told me, "You're just a big baby. You're worthless and make trouble for me, and are just like your mother." I cried every single day and longed to be with my mother and daddy. My grandmother was abusive and wicked to me verbally, emotionally, and psychologically. That abuse left scars on me for life. At the tender and innocent age of only six years old, I had no clue that I was being sucker punched repeatedly by a person who should have loved me and whom I could have loved and trusted. Instead, all I felt was hurt and agony. That profound pain wounded my heart, soul, and my very existence. That's what it felt like to be sucker punched at six years of age.

The Pain Continued Throughout Adolescence

My brother and I reunited with our parents and siblings the

middle of my first grade year in elementary school. I walked to school every morning with my older brother in Overland Park, Kansas (providing another opportunity to bully me). I heard comments such as, "Why doesn't your mother drive you to school?" We even walked in the rain and snow. I, for one, never even considered why my mother didn't drive us to school simply because we were able to walk that short distance. Nevertheless, we were bullied for walking.

I felt extreme prejudice because I was the only girl in the all-inclusive white, elementary school with red hair and freckles. I was a freak. Red heads constituted only four percent of the population in the entire United States at that time. I was the last one chosen for sports. When we played dodge ball, the other children targeted me outwardly and tortured me. They threw that ball at me so hard it hurt my little thirty-four-pound body. I would go into the bathroom afterward and cry. I was the last one chosen in class for partner projects and the only one not selected as a bunk-mate during those years at summer camp.

I remember a scrawny girl named Jonie in the fourth through sixth grades who made quirky noises all the time. Her father was a doctor. In my Camp Fire Girls' Group, she and I were the only ones who never had friends. She didn't like me because I was ugly and I didn't like her because she made strange, peculiar, bird-like sounds. You'd have thought we would've stuck together like glue, but we didn't. When she missed meetings during the week, I listened as they picked on Jonie and laughed right along with them. But when she showed up the next week, my name was thrown in the bucket, too. The others called us names and sucker punched us at every meeting we had.

Jonie never went to the week-long summer camps, but I did. It was pure hell. I hated being the only one not having a bunk-mate during those days. I even had to sleep in another group's cabin. Every time I turned around, I was sucker punched as a kid, both in school and out of school. So, you see, for me it lasted for many years as I grew up.

For my own thirteenth birthday party, twelve girls attended. We lived in the country at that time and had two horses. The girls at school knew they'd be able to go horseback riding and play pool. I cried at my own thirteenth birthday party because everyone had a partner during the games and even had a partner to play pool with, except me—and it was my party! I was so hurt and upset that I cried to my mother. She told me to go back outside and have fun. How do you have fun when all of the others are ignoring you at your own party and making fun of you on top of that? My parents never understood how sucker punched I felt from the ages of six through thirteen.

Junior high was even more of a nightmare because everyone was "hooking up" except me because I was perceived as being so ugly. I only went to one school dance where I was the wallflower. Name-calling was an everyday occurrence. I dreaded going to school. I avoided any extra-curricular activities. I got involved with the wrong crowd when I was thirteen to fourteen years old so that I could finally fit in and feel accepted by a select few. Thankfully, I quickly realized the poor choice I'd made and got out of that crowd once we moved again to a different town.

Understanding the Feelings and Significance of Being Sucker Punched

I never realized that all the times I was sucker punched as a child and teenager were preparing me for what was to come later in life. You see, although I cried often and my heart hurt terribly, and I was not happy as a little girl, I was able to handle all that stress quite well. My family was strict, with Christian values, and my safe haven was at home and at our church. I never felt threatened with being sucker punched and did not even realize until right this very moment as I am typing these words that home and church were my sanctuaries away from the stress. I looked forward to church on Wednesday nights and Sunday mornings at church followed by family dinners. There was never any question about what we were going to do on Sundays. We went to church, came home, had our big meal at 1:00 PM, and then did our homework if we had any. We had a consistent schedule throughout the week. My mother made sure of this.

Bullies or Beauties to Others—It's Your Choice

There are two consequences to being sucker punched repeatedly during childhood and adolescence. The first is that you can become a bully yourself. You might become cold, hardened, and hateful toward others as you grow up, and perhaps even develop abnormal personality disorders, such as becoming depressed or a sociopath, or suffering from personality disorders.

The second is that you can become very sensitive to others and the world around them. This is what happened to me. After being sucker punched at the innocent age of six and throughout my adolescent years, I knew firsthand what it felt like to be the victim of bullying. By the time I was fifteen, I was the one who always stood up for others when they were picked on. I became compassionate, concerned, and kind as a result of being sucker punched. By the time I was twenty-two, I was involved in five civic and community organizations, all of which benefited children.

Now We Know What Sucker Punched
Means and Feels Like

I've been sucker punched right in the gut many times in the past, but now those blows will be thrown elsewhere. I have a system in place that works for me and it can work for you, too. Later in this book, I'll teach you how to dodge those who are targeting you so you'll avoid being sucker punched again in the future, or at the very least, not quite as often. Seriously, there is a simple method. In this book, I'll show you how to keep that Sucker Punched Syndrome™ (SPS) at bay.

Dialogue to Contemplate Through Directed Journaling:

❖ *What is your first memory of being sucker punched? This may be upsetting, but try to recall the very first time. Now can you remember the second, and the third? What were they?*

❖ *Did it feel bad and hurt you, or were you able to just shrug it off at that time? Why or why not?*

❖ *If you are raising children or grandchildren, or have neighbors, and saw someone getting sucker punched, would you be hesitant to get involved? Why or why not? What would you do?*

❖ *How can we teach others that it is not okay to bully anyone?*

❖ *What can we say to others to help them understand that nasty and insidious words can leave deep, harmful, emotional, and psychological scars that may last a lifetime?*

CHAPTER 2

Dating, Love, and Relationships are Not Immune From the Agony

"Do newly dating couples get to have all the sex? Is a one-night-stand worth it? Is there more than one kind of love? What makes someone desirable? Quite often, the very thing that you found attractive about your mate in the first place is not the same thing that you will find attractive ten to twenty years later. Research has shown that we do not fall into love—we grow into love. If a couple stays married for twenty-plus years, the chances of their marriage lasting a lifetime are very good. I've been sucker punched in the dating world, in my love life, and in some of my relationships. Love does make the world go around and is bliss. So, I will continue my journey of chance and see where the winding road leads me."

~ Dr. Gayle Joplin Hall.

Dating is a Full Time Job—Perhaps It Should Be Classified as a Sport

I don't know what your experiences with dating are, but I am here to say that it's a full-time job when you're in the market and are "shopping." I have a saying (there are so many), that goes like this: "The shopping bag is open or it is closed. I am looking or I am not." You need to know what you're searching for, and quite often, this is where the problem lies in the first place. Unless you know what you want, how can you ever be satisfied with the date you end up with? Do you want a real date, someone you can possibly relate to, build a friendship with, carry on a conversation with, and perhaps fall in love with and marry? Or are you looking for a one-night stand—someone you can have sex with and then never see again? You must know what you're looking for. As a Relationship and Lifestyle Coach, and one who has studied human behavior for over twenty years, I am here to tell you that most of the time, people simply don't know what they want.

Dating takes much effort. Let's face it, when you're walking out the door for a first date, you're putting on your best face and trying to impress. At least, this would be my guess. I never did that. In fact, when I used online dating sites for over four years, I posted a less than flattering photo of myself so when the men would meet me they would be pleasantly surprised. I also didn't go to any extreme measures on the first date to be glamorous. I showed up looking like "just me." I wanted them to know that this was how I was in "real life" and they could take me or leave me. Unfortunately for my dates, I had a ten-minute rule. If when first meeting a man I knew that I would not see him again because of misrepresentation on his part, I would not even sit down, order a drink, or anything. I simply stated, "I am so sorry, but I have been misled by the pictures you posted, so I feel deceived. I must go now. Thank you for your time." I had to deliver the dreadful sucker punch to the man. This actually happened many times. I'm not proud of that, but why waste his time, or mine? I felt terrible for hurting his feelings, but knew I was doing the right thing for me. I stayed true to myself.

Settling for Rotten Eggs

So many people, women and men included, have such low self-worth and low self-esteem they'll settle for anyone or go on any date, just to keep from being alone. I was guilty of this not so long ago and am not very proud to admit it. I'm revealing my soul in this book, so I can help you avoid making some of the same mistakes I've made. I settled for rotten eggs, and made the same mistakes time and time again, when I was certain that the men I dated were not the men I wanted to spend the rest of my life with. They were not worthy of me, they did not share my value system, and they did not appreciate nor recognize the uniqueness and qualities of the person I am. How many of you reading this know the exact same thing about the rotten egg you're dating right this minute? You need to get those rotten eggs out of your life and out of your home before they stink up your entire house.

Let's Talk About Sex, Baby: Don't Get Worked Up About This—It's One of Life's Greatest Pleasures

Just reading or hearing the word "sex" makes some people cringe. I've never quite figured this out. When I was a Psychology Professor, our classroom discussions on sex were some of the most interesting of all. In some of my classes, we would hold panel discussions related to dating, love, marriage, and divorce. It was grand because everyone learned from each other. I pre-selected students in different age groups (from eighteen to sixty-seven) and privately wrote to them to ask them to be on the panel. I also asked for volunteers from the class. Many times, there were far too many participants, so I carefully had to select those I felt would best be able to act as our "expert panel guests" on these subjects.

Surprisingly, some of the younger students were conservative in their views on sex, while others stated "hooking up" and "one night stands" were normal. Undoubtedly, the most shocking sex story was told by a woman in her late fifties. She was a grandmotherly-type we'd all grown to love having in the class. During the panel discussion, she informed us that she'd been married for thirty-five years to her husband and had the same boyfriend for over twenty years. The three of them shared a home together and she chose whom to sleep with and when. We laughed and learned in the best way. We held nothing back. Students from other classes approached me, wanting to know when they could sign up to take my classes.

On a negative note, many girls stated they were used for sex and then dumped after putting out. This is such an old story that I am really astonished any female would not already be aware of this when she has sex on a first date with someone she really likes. How many times have we heard this same story? The guy gets the girl. He flatters and compliments her. He takes her out for dinner, or perhaps doesn't even do that. She willingly has sex. He takes her home and she never gets a call from him again. When she passes him in the hallways at school, he scoffs at her. She's just been sucker punched. Yes, that hurts. Why wouldn't it?

Sex is sex when you "grow up" also. It amazes me how many women on the social media scene brag openly about how they "want it, need it, and are going to have sex whenever they want to with any man they want to without feeling guilty." The line used is, "men have done it for centuries, so why can't we?" Every day, on facebook and on other online sites, women call themselves "relationship and sex experts" who have no credentials at all, other than bragging rights of having slept with multitudes of men. I hate to be the one to explain this to you, but sweeties, this doesn't make you experts. This just means you're cheap. These same "experts" wonder why they can't get good, quality men interested in them, other than "just for sex."

I can get more men interested in me by just walking through a room because I am witty, beautiful, and sexy, without acting or talking cheap. Let's face it. If you cheapen and devalue yourself, why would any man want you for his life partner? A slut is a slut. Slutty girls attract low quality, hot guys. For fun sex, be a slut and hook up. For even more fun sex, find a partner you can love and he will become your hot lover as you teach him what you want and need in bed. I was taught to be a lady. Therefore, I'll never divulge the number of men I've slept with, you won't see me in pictures looking like I've just been laid, and I won't brag about the hot guy I "banged" last night. I have more self-respect than that and I ask women to remember their feminine traits and be "ladies" so men can be men. Let him hunt you first—then he will treasure you.

Love Hurts—Remember That Song?

Love is not supposed to hurt, but there are times when you're sucker punched in the gut so hard, you wonder if you'll ever recover from the blow. My guess is that for anyone and practically everyone reading this book, each of you has been sucker punched at least once from the loss of love. It hurts having your heart broken and during that time, it's difficult to imagine you'll pull through. This is when you call in your support team and rally the troops or girlfriends for help.

Is love an action or is love just a word? What do you think? The very famous Dr. Randy Pausch, who gave his Last Lecture at Carnegie Mellon University in September 2007 (before dying of pancreatic cancer at the age of forty-seven), stated to his baby daughter one thing about boys, men, and love. He said, "Believe nothing a man tells you and everything a man shows you." I love this advice and if only I had known this when I was "shopping" for a man, this could have saved me from being sucker punched in love. Words are cheap and actions speak volumes. Love doesn't always have to hurt. Every so often, love can be magical.

Kissing the Frogs and Squelching the Icky Toads

We've all kissed our share of frogs and I've crushed many toads on the hunt for love and the perfect relationship. I'm embarrassed by how many men's hearts I've broken along the way. I never misled any man. I was direct with each of them. I've been sucker punched by three. Yes—only three men in my entire lifetime have sucker punched me, so perhaps this is fortunate since I have kissed many frogs along the way. I know very few people who've been fortunate enough to find their life-long mate without kissing those frogs, stomping out those toads, or putting up with the bitches along the journey in finding their king or queen. If you found your mate without that drama, consider yourself one of the privileged. My own parents have been married fifty-nine years. I always thought that would be my life too, but I have not been so fortunate. Please continue reading.

Who Hasn't Been Sucker Punched in a Relationship?

As I just mentioned, my parents have been married for fifty-nine years without arguing, lying, or disliking each other. In fact, they are more loving toward each other than any other couple I know, even newlyweds. Do you want to know why? My parents enjoy what the majority of couples are never able to achieve in their marriages—Consummate Love. There is more than one kind of love. Sternberg's Model of Love states that complete love must be composed of all three necessary components for a successful marriage. Consummate Love consists of intimacy, passion, and commitment.

I've been personally sucker punched through infatuation in one relationship; empty love in a marriage where there was no intimacy or passion; and romantic love, where I had physical and emotional attraction, but no commitment. Two of my marriages ended due to my husbands' infidelity.

My limit is cheating in a marriage. I will be second-class to no other woman because I value myself more than that. One of my marriages failed after seventeen years, when my husband told me he'd been having an affair with the same woman for over five years. He said he needed to "get this off his chest." He chose to tell me this news on New Year's Day. I was at the car wash and he followed me there. Well, he got hosed and I divorced him within five months, although he pleaded and begged me not to do so.

I was the perfect wife and mother to his children and well respected in the community. His sucker punching me was so humiliating. I didn't think I could recover from the pain of having to tell my parents that I was divorcing the man they thought was so nice. He hadn't been so nice to me, when I was home taking care of his children and taking care of the household while he was being a playboy. Karma is a bitch, because the woman he married after me turned out to be a great big liar who cheated on him with many men, got pregnant (after telling him she could never get pregnant), and then proceeded to harass him during and after his divorce. I was the good wife, she was the trophy wife, and karma just sucks. Although I truly wish him no harm ever, it was ironic that the person he chose to be with cheated on him in a more embarrassing way than he had ever cheated on me. He royally got sucker punched.

Love is Worth the Wait and Underpriced: Know Your Value

Again, this goes right back to knowing what you want out of the relationship and knowing your worth. Until you value yourself as a person, you will continue to get sucker punched and make poor choices in a mate. You must learn to be happy with yourself as a person before you can bring anything to another person or to a relationship. This is how and why most relationships fail. I'm speaking from experience. It took me so long to understand that I needed to find happiness within myself, instead of hoping to find happiness from any new relationship. You just might be able to keep the Sucker Punched Syndrome™ (SPS) down to a bare minimum if you learn this about yourself first.

Directed Journaling

❖ If you are in the dating scene, what are the criteria you use for finding dates? Do you have a "method" you follow? Why or why not? What is the method? How has this worked for you?

❖ Why have you made the same mistakes in dating, love, or in your relationships? Could you have avoided being sucker punched if you'd realized that you chose some of those people to fulfill empty places within your soul? Do you believe this to be true? Why or why not?

❖ How important is sex to you in your dating, relationships, or married life? What can you do to change this aspect if it's not going well? Do you think a relationship or marriage should be broken if the sex life is gone? Is this a personal choice, or one a Lifestyle Coach might be able to help you work on with your partner?

❖ Is monogamous sex conceivable in this decade? Are you capable of having a committed relationship? If so, why do so many marriages end in divorce? How can we change this for ourselves and as a society, or should we be concerned? Has there been a clear distinction of roles since the sexual revolution in the late 1960's?

❖ Do you believe it's promising to have a strong love filled with intimacy, passion, and commitment (Consummate Love) in this day and age? How do you find a suitable mate, if you don't have one? Why is our society so directed at "couples" rather than satisfied with single people?

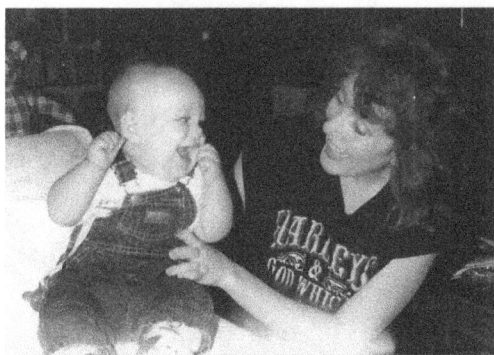

CHAPTER 3

Domestic Violence—My Worse Sucker Punched Nightmare of All (Feeling Homeless in My Own Home)

"He hovered over me, standing on our own bed, as I was awakened from sleeping. I woke up feeling the breath being sucked out of me. I was being suffocated with a pillow. I heard laughter. This was my husband, the one who only four days prior, told me he would love me forever. He promised to take care of me and our baby (who I was six weeks pregnant with at the time of our marriage). He stood there on the bed, as I lay as still as I could, crying, and wondering what I had done to deserve this mad man. I was threatened to never speak with another man, ordered to dissolve my successful advertising business, and told that 'he could make me disappear at any moment and nobody would ever know the cause of my death,' since he was a Pathologist. I lived in constant fear for the next seven years."

~ Dr. Gayle Joplin Hall.

Domestic Violence Explained in Simple Terms

Although women have been victimized throughout centuries, society has only recently addressed this sensitive subject. L.E. Walker was the pioneer in this field and studied hundreds of women in the late 1970's with her team of professionals. The description for domestic violence is behavior characterized by the exploitation of power and control by one person over another who is or who has been in an intimate relationship. Walker described this violence as abuse when a partner or ex-partner attempts to physically, emotionally, or psychologically dominate the other person. A battered woman is the person in the relationship abused by her partner. In ninety-five percent of all cases of domestic violence, the woman is the victim of abuse and the batterer is the man. Domestic violence can also happen in same-sex relationships. Moreover, men can be the victims of domestic violence. Nevertheless, statistically, women are the primary victims of this repugnant crime.

Three Distinct Phases in Patterns of Domestic Violence Include Getting Sucker Punched During Phase One and Two

In order to understand domestic violence, one must understand the three phases that make up this cycle of violence. The preliminary phase is tension building, sometimes known as "walking on eggshells." Women have described this feeling as "never knowing when the rage may begin or what may set off her mate in a fit of anger." The abuse may be verbal threats, such as humiliation, name-calling, screaming, or yelling. This could include psychological abuse such as threats to leave. At times, there could be minor physical violence during phase one of this cycle of tension building. This could last for hours, or possibly even days.

The second phase in the cycle of violence is when the batter-er may become either physically or sexually violent. This is the acute phase. Physical violence is exactly what it sounds like—beatings, choking, breaking bones, punching, slapping, using a weapon, restraining, etc. Additionally, the victim may not be allowed to use the bathroom, eat, or sleep.

The final phase in the cycle of violence is known as the "honeymoon period." The batterer promises he will not harm his victim again. He seems remorseful, may bring gifts and is charming, asks for forgiveness, and at times, may even act as though nothing ever occurred in the first place. Within days, the cycle of violence could repeat itself all over again. For me, in my domestic violent situation, I lived in this reign of terror on a nightly basis.

Domestic Violence is a Nauseating Expression

I was visiting with a dear colleague. I asked if I could speak at any of my friend's civic or church groups on the subject of domestic violence (DV) during the month of October. October is National Domestic Violence Awareness Month. The response was, "We really don't want to talk about something like that, Gayle. It just isn't pleasant." I was shocked. Hell, no, it's not pleasant! It's ghastly, and part of the problem is that the general population still wants to keep it behind closed doors and act like it doesn't exist. We simply must be willing to talk about it. I'm going to shed my attire and expose it all by disclosing what domestic violence is and how sucker punched I was from DV, more times than I care to remember or count.

Pregnant, Four Days, and Already a Victim
of Domestic Violence

In the opening quote, I explained how I was awakened by being suffocated by a pillow and hearing laughter. My new husband soared six feet over me in our bed, while I laid there choking for air. This is a true story, as is everything else I am writing in my book. I knew domestic violence existed and had heard of women getting beat up, but always thought they deserved it for cheating on their husbands, being scumbags, or for other reasons. I never dreamed this could happen to *me*, a normal, successful, smart, and beautiful woman.

The rage from my husband, who was drunk at the time of the domestic violence, lasted for at least two hours. He finally fell asleep and when he did, I crept downstairs to the family room, and crawled up on the sofa and just cried. I knew I was going to tell my partner in business about what had happened, but also realized I could not tell anyone else. I felt shame. Yes, I was ashamed that this had happened to me. This is why people don't seek help immediately when they are abused. They are filled with shame and think they deserve this abuse, for whatever reason. I told only one person what had happened to me the next day. This was my secret. You see, we are very good at keeping secrets.

Forced to Move From My Home—
Making Out With the Movers

Yes, I was forced to sell the home I lived in so that my new husband and I could move to another home, one that I had not shared with my previous husband who I had been married to for 17 years. My husband couldn't stand the idea of living in a home where any other man had previously lived with me, so he

forced me to sell my home. I was in my first trimester of pregnancy, and was experiencing the tiredness that so often accom-
panies the first trimester. Yet, here I was, packing up an entire
house to move a couple of miles away to a brand new builder's
show house. My new husband promised me the life of a queen
if I married him; the same husband who got me pregnant and
hovered over me only four days after I married him. The one who
frightened me so dreadfully that I sought counsel to see if I could
get my marriage annulled. Unfortunately, I could not do so.

The movers came as planned on the scheduled day of the
move. I had worked for nearly an entire month, setting up our
brand new home, so that only the large pieces of furniture and
extremely heavy things needed to be moved by the professional
movers. When my new husband could not reach me by telephone, he accused me of being a slut. (This was before everyone had cell phones in their hands at all times.)

He showed up at the new house after work at 5:30 PM and
yelled at me out in the driveway, calling me all kinds of names.
Our new neighbors heard and saw him behaving like a fool.
I was so mortified. I simply went into the house after paying
the movers. My husband accused me of sleeping with all three
of the movers. He chased me for hours from room to room in
this beautiful, new home of 3500 square feet. Up and down
three flights of stairs I ran, as he ranted and carried on with this
wild behavior and name calling for hours. I was exhausted, just
from the day of moving, and wanted nothing more than to go
to bed and sleep. I remember him passing out in the middle of
the huge bathroom floor around 4:00 AM. Our bathroom was
the size of most families' living rooms. It was gigantic. I just left
him there, climbed into my bed, and cried. I knew my life was
going to be hell.

My Beautiful Baby Boy Should Be Just a Joy

My son was beautiful even before he was born. I was sucker punched from the minute I walked into the house carrying my precious bundle in my arms. Since he was my last child, I desperately wanted to nurse him, but after five days of practically starving my baby, I surrendered to the fact it was not working and gave him a bottle of formula. He sucked it right down and stopped crying. My husband was extremely jealous of the time I spent with our new baby. It was as though he was competing with this tiny, priceless little boy, as though he was a baby himself. If I had been a psychology major at that time, I would've recognized that my husband never had the nurturing or care he needed as a baby and young child. Therefore, he never felt the comfort of trust vs. mistrust, as Erikson points out in our important first stage of life during infancy.

Backpacks, Bottles, and Booze

I coddled my infant son from the minute he was born because he was so beautiful to me, but mostly, because I knew he would be my last baby. Everything he did, every sound he made, every time he rolled over or grinned, was recorded on video. I was in awe of this little bundle of joy. He brought me so much love and happiness. My baby particularly liked to be in his backpack while I cooked dinner every night. He would grab onto my long hair and chew on it (I know it sounds gross, but my baby loved doing that!) while I worked in the kitchen.

One hot summer night in June, my husband came home—angry from the minute he walked in the door. He asked me what we were having for dinner. I told him that I was fixing what he asked me to prepare when we had talked earlier on the telephone that afternoon. As we sat down at the table to eat, he

26

grumbled about how much trouble I was, how miserable his life was, how much he hated his job, and how fat I was (my size 6 was fat!). He asked me why I had to constantly have the baby in the room making cooing sounds as we were trying to eat (my baby was three and a half months old at the time). My husband kept complaining, which soon turned into yelling at me about how I could not cook, how I could not take care of myself, and how I was a slob and was still fat. How could I be fat if I wore a size 6 dress and was in fantastic shape?

This was all so comical, because I was getting up and riding a bicycle every morning seven miles before he was ever out of bed, pulling my baby in a protected cart behind me on my bicycle. I went to the gym for two hours every afternoon to work out and at the age of thirty-six, looked better than I had in my entire life. Yet, my husband was telling me that I was fat, never fixed myself up, and looked like a slob. I began to cry, as I picked up my baby, who was starting to fuss from all the yelling my husband was dishing out. As I leaned over to pick up the baby, I got a whiff of my husband's breath. He had been drinking and not just a little bit. He reeked of alcohol.

Flying Spaghetti on the Wall

The next thing I knew, my husband picked up his plate of spaghetti and slammed it against the kitchen wall. He threw that plate almost eight feet, so you can imagine the mess flying spaghetti makes as it breezes its way through the air before it splats against the wall. As he stormed out of the kitchen, I began to clean up the mess before he came back in, because I knew there would be more from him—more verbal abuse, more harsh words, more yelling and screaming, more humiliation, and God knew what else. Within an hour, while wearing my trusty backpack with precious cargo onboard, I cleaned up the mess and put my kitchen back in order. I heard those heavy footsteps coming up the stairs as I laid my baby down to sleep in his pint-sized crib in my bedroom.

The Cycles of Violence: Phases One and Two

During the next five hours, I was cursed and screamed at, pushed down with one finger, knocked across the room with two fingers (so hard that I skidded on my butt), and chased around the house while being name-called. I watched as the phones were ripped out of the wall in every room when I tried to dial 911. He yanked me by the arm from room-to-room and made me watch as he ripped out the phone lines. I tried to grab my keys and baby so I could leave in the car, even though I only had on a bra and a pair of shorts. My husband called me a slut and a whore and finally locked me in the bedroom, where I sank to the floor in a lifeless heap and cried.

I contemplated jumping off the twenty-foot deck that overlooked the patio of our room, but realized I might break my legs during the fall. I also knew there would be nobody to care for my three-and-a-half month-old baby if I hurt myself. After five hours of this nonsense, otherwise known as phase one and two of the cycles of violence, I convinced my husband that I would be a better wife, so he let me out of the bedroom.

The baby was still sleeping in his little crib in my room. I quickly glanced at him, said a rapid prayer, and asked God to protect him. Amazingly, my precious baby had slept throughout this entire ordeal, and I believed God would guard him during my next decision. I wanted out of there and that was all I could think of. I would come back for my baby. I had to believe my husband would not hurt my baby, since he had not laid a hand on him ever before during a domestic violent occurrence.

Half-Naked in the Neighborhood

With my husband still standing right next to me, I bolted for the front door. All I could think of was getting away from this mad man and calling the police to help me, to help my baby, and to get out of the mess we were in. I made it out of the house wearing only a pair of baggy shorts and a bra—nothing else. I had no shirt or shoes on, my hair was in a sloppy pony tail, and my mascara was smeared all over my face from crying. I was not a pretty sight. I took off running through the neighborhood, with my husband screaming at me and running behind me.

I have no clue where my strength to run came from, except the divine grace of God Himself. I looked back once, and saw that my husband was starting to give up the chase, as he finally shrieked, "Why are you running away from me, Gayle? I'm not going to hurt you. I love you." I kept on running until I got around to the next block in our neighborhood. It was almost midnight. Very few houses had their inside lights on and a limited number had their outside lights on.

I approached the first house with outside lights on and quickly rang the doorbell. I saw a woman peek out the front window through the curtains and then heard her as she spoke to her husband who also came and peeked at me standing there on the front porch, half-naked. They didn't answer the door. I said loudly, "I need your help. Please dial 911 for me." I waited for about thirty seconds and then left when I realized they weren't going to help me. After being assaulted by my husband and stalked for hours, I was now being sucker punched by neighbors and their refusal to help me, based on the way I looked!

Fearfully, I ran until I came to the next house with the outside lights on. I was running through the neighborhood because I knew that at any moment, my husband would come and hunt me down. He had not done this before, just as I had not run half-naked through an upscale neighborhood in a populated metropolitan city before. Nevertheless, I had this gut feeling that I was going to be sucker punched again, out in the street, if he caught me. I was very frightened. I wanted and needed help from someone—anyone.

I walked up the stairs to the second house with the outside lights on and rang the doorbell. Someone inside the house turned off the outside lights. I couldn't believe it! I'd just been sucker punched again, right in the gut. Apparently, someone inside the house had seen me standing there with my makeup smeared all over my face and wearing only a bra and a pair of shorts, and decided to not help me. I began to cry, but as I did, I was more determined than ever to get this husband of mine put in jail at least for the night for what he had done to me.

The third house with outside lights on looked familiar to me. It was about four blocks from where we lived. Some people were playing cards in the living room and when the door was answered, I realized that this home was where my thirteen-year-old came to visit with a friend sometimes. The homeowners recognized me as "the mother of . . ." and quickly invited me in. I asked them to dial 911. They brought me a shirt to put on and handed me the telephone. Just as I was making the call, I glanced out and saw the headlights of the custom van we owned approaching the house. I screamed into the phone, "It's him, it's him! Please hurry and come, I am afraid of him." The police arrived within one minute.

My husband circled around again, most likely because of all the cars parked around this particular house. He must have known this is where I was. As I saw the police cars approaching from the opposite direction, I was unafraid and ran out into the street with the male owner of the home. I told them I had made the call. They asked me if my husband was armed and I told them he could be, since he owned many weapons. I informed them he had been drinking all night and had harassed me, assaulted me, and locked me in my room. They forced him to stop his vehicle, threw him on the ground, and cuffed him. He looked up at me and kept asking, "Gayle, what are you doing to me?"

He was booked on a charge of assault. The police officers in the other car took me home and informed me that they could charge me with child abandonment for leaving my baby alone in the house. After completely explaining my story, and telling the officers that I had to flee but had every intention of coming back to get my baby, they realized I was telling the truth. When I walked in the front door of my home, my baby was still asleep.

I woke my baby when I picked him up because I was kissing him so much. His little jammies were drenched with sweat. Even as tiny as he was, he must have known that his mother was in trouble that hot, summer night in her own home. I gave him a bath, fed him a bottle, and put him in my bed with me. By this time, it was 2:00 AM. June 27 is forever a flashbulb memory planted in my mind.

Cycle of Violence: Phase Three, the Honeymoon Period

My husband's brother bailed him out of jail the next morning and he was back in my home early. I was very scared to see him. While his older brother was there, he was apologetic, begged me to stay with him when I told him I was going to file for divorce, and promised it would never happen again. He told me that he didn't know what had gotten into him.

The minute my husband's older brother left, he started in on me with harsh words. He was furious that there was an assault charge against him. He kept saying, "If I'd wanted to really hurt you, I could've really hurt you. I could kill you like a fly, Gayle." My "honeymoon phase" in the cycle of violence lasted less than two hours before the first cycle began again. Thankfully, he left for work. The minute he was gone, I had the phone book out and called counselors who referred me to local women's shelters. I chose the closest one to my home that was only ten miles away.

A Battered Woman—Is This Me?

As I drove to the women's shelter, I wondered how it would be. The woman I spoke with on the phone asked me if I had a police report or anything from the police department that I could give her when I arrived. It made me feel as though they wouldn't take my word or didn't believe me. I carried my infant son in my arms as I walked through those double doors that morning, the day following the arrest of my husband for terrorizing me in my own home.

I sat down and began filling out many required papers about my family income, how long this type of abuse had been occurring in the home, and other self-report measures. The intake person told me I would meet with a counselor on staff, after I gave her my police record from the night before. As we began talking in the private room, I had an eerie feeling about it all that is difficult to describe. She used the term, "battered woman" when describing me and I did not like the sound of it.

The counselor told me I was wrong for leaving my baby

when I fled the house and said she could call Child Protective Services and have my baby removed from me for doing so. I was scared silly. I told her that I'd be a better wife and not let my husband harm me or my baby. The counselor advised that I needed to be concerned about myself first, but my ears were closed because her words resonated about ". . . having my baby removed from me . . ." Nothing else she said the rest of the time was even heard or acknowledged. I couldn't get out of there quickly enough.

Living in a Car, Hiding From the World, Feeling Homeless, and Full of Shame

After leaving the women's shelter, I strapped my baby into the back seat of the car and headed for home. I was flooded with emotions, feeling depressed, sad, angry, and guilty about leaving my baby asleep in his crib the night before as my husband chased and abused me. After learning that the counselor could make a call and have my precious baby taken from me I wanted to hide from women's shelters. What good were they, if they couldn't help me?

I couldn't go home to my beautiful, custom-made house and go through that hell again, because my husband was still filled with rage. I couldn't call my parents after having tried to speak with them about these problems earlier in my marriage. I didn't want to bring the family even more shame by going through yet another divorce and knew the reason for the divorce wouldn't matter. I couldn't tell my friends because they all had happy marriages or were divorced and didn't want me and my new baby in their homes. I couldn't check into any hotel, for fear that my husband would search every hotel registry until he found me. I had nowhere to run and nowhere to hide.

I was frightened beyond words.

The cash I kept hidden in my purse was going to have to be enough to last me for a while. I never made it home that day. My infant son and I stayed in our car. I believed if we found a place to park, we'd just stay in the car and not be discovered. There'd be no way for my husband to phone me; find me; yell, name call, push or knock me down; or barricade me in my car if he didn't know where I was with my baby. I told nobody where I was going and drove around for an hour, looking for the perfect place to park.

Since I only had my purse and a diaper bag with me, I went to the store to buy diapers, wipes, and formula for my baby. I also bought a pillow, blanket, and a piece of bride's netting to throw over us for when we would be sleeping in the car. Once I decided where to park the car, I was no longer afraid.

The first night was fine. I was proud of myself. The second day, after sleeping in the car all night on June 28, we went into a mall and just spent the day there. I watched people and pushed my baby in his stroller that I always kept in the trunk of my car. As darkness set in, I became scared. I worried that the batteries in my flashlight might burn out (I've been afraid of the dark since I was six years old). I curled up in the back seat with my happy baby and thought how beautiful that God makes children so they don't remember anything until about the age of three.

On the third day of feeling homeless and still feeling absent from the world, my baby was not feeling well. He was fussing and crying, and not his usual pleasant self. His smile was gone. He needed me to rock him and sing to him. I took him to a furniture store where I could rock him and even told the sales person I just needed to rock my baby. She told me to "take my time." After two hours, we went back to the mall, were I could push the stroller in the comfort of air conditioning. The third night was hell for my baby. He cried most of the night and nothing I did made him happy. That's when I knew he was getting an ear infection.

The final day of fleeing from my home, sleeping in my car, and trying to take care of a baby in the back seat of a car where the temperature was eighty-five degrees, I took the baby to the doctor. He confirmed that my baby had an ear infection and needed antibiotics. My son hated those drops in the mouth and disliked the ear drops as well. He was cranky and miserable.

I tried to tell the pediatrician that I'd been abused by an associate and friend of his, someone in the business, but he didn't acknowledge what I told him, nor did he ask me any questions about the domestic violence or if I was okay. Worse, the pediatrician didn't even ask if the baby had been harmed by my husband. I later thought about how odd it was that a pediatrician didn't ask that question, and yet at the women's shelter, I was threatened with having my baby taken away.

Entering the House of Terror

I knew that I had to go back home and was terrified of what I was going to face as I walked in the door. Amazingly, my husband didn't even ask me where I'd been. I don't know if he'd tried to find me, or whether he'd been on a drinking binge the entire four days and passed out and not gone to work, or what'd he'd done while I was gone. But not once did he ask me where I'd been.

Two days after I returned home, the emotional and psychological abuse started all over again. I lived in hell for the next several years and started building a firm plan to get out for good.

It took me a very long time to leave because of shame, blame, and guilt. I finally left after seven years. Many more stories will be told in another book, devoted to domestic violence.

Directed Journaling

❖ *Can you explain the three phases in the cycle of violence? Do you have preconceived stereotypes of what a person must look like to be a victim of domestic violence? Why might this be a form of being sucker punched?*

❖ *Have you ever considered being in a domestic violent relationship, or knowing someone who is in this situation, as being sucker punched? Why or why not? Is this due to lack of information about the meaning of domestic violence? What can we do to change this in our society?*

❖ *How important is counseling from a trained professional in helping a victim of domestic violence? Should marriage or couples counseling ever be considered when there is violence in the home? (The answer to this is "Heck, NO!") Would you seek counseling if you were living with a situation where domestic violence occurred? Why or why not?*

❖ *Should training of police officers and first responders include courses on domestic violence so they understand the dynamics involved? Why or why not? Would you be shocked to learn that not all hospital emergency room personnel and intake clerks are aware of the dangers of domestic violence? Would you be surprised to learn that 50 percent of the time, the nurse on staff will ask the woman (victim) right in front of the man (batterer) how she got that black eye and those broken ribs? How can a victim respond if the batterer is standing in the room? She can't respond—or can she?*

❖ *What, if anything, has ever made you feel like you cannot go* home? Have you ever felt homeless? Have you ever actually been homeless? Please explain in detail. Have you ever slept in your car or on the street? How did that make you feel? Did you feel full of shame and guilt? What can we do as a society to conquer homelessness?

CHAPTER 4

You're Fired! Those Words Resonate a Long Time, Like a Low Blow to the Belly

"You're fired! It's really hard to get over hearing those words once you've had them bounce off your ears. I've been fired a total of four times in my entire life. The first time, I was only thirteen years old and worked in a corn field, detasseling corn. I was fired for being too short. The second time I was twenty-one and this story is the one I'm going to tell. I chose this story because it's the one most people will relate to. I suppose some people know when they are very young exactly what they want to do when they grow up. However, it wasn't that way for me. My life unfolded during my late forties. Read this chapter, even if you've never been fired."

~ Dr. Gayle Joplin Hall.

Brand New Marriage, New Baby, New Town, and Our Own House—Now What?

I was only eighteen when I got married six months after high school. My parents didn't think it was a great idea, but of course I thought that I knew more than they did. I didn't know what else to do, except to get married and have a baby, living in the small town where I was. I hated school, so the thought of going to college never even crossed my mind. I wasn't wildly in love with the boy I dated my senior year of high school, but I thought love would grow. Fifteen months after I married, I gave birth to my first child. Within two hours of giving birth, my husband left me to go back to his job, a hundred and fifty miles away. I never got over that separation. The birth was a difficult one and I almost died. Who dies in childbirth in this day and age? My doctor said I shouldn't have any more children (although I did give birth to two more babies).

Within three weeks of giving birth to my first child, my best friend from high school helped me pack up my entire house so that I could move to be with my husband. We hauled our meager possessions and household items a hundred fifty miles to our new home in a horse trailer, as neighbors looked on. We were flat broke, so we did what we had to do. I was humiliated beyond tears.

There I was in a new town with no friends, no family, and a brand new baby to take care of. My husband worked long hours, so I rarely saw him. I wanted so desperately to be independent that I decided to get a "real" job. Once I located a babysitter I studied the newspaper week after week, applying for many secretarial jobs. My skills included transcription, typing, and administrative support. My spirits were running at an all time low. For the first time in my life, I was facing adult depression and desperation, although I had no idea about what was wrong with me at the time.

I Got the Job! I Got the Job!

Just as I was ready to throw in the towel and give up on ever finding a job, I received a call from an executive secretary who worked for a national insurance company headquartered in our small town. My interview session was for 2:00 PM the following day. In my gut, I knew I was going to land this job.

A big, bold "visitors" parking sign greeted me as I pulled up to the massive building. My hands were sweaty as I got out of the car, yet, I was still confident. From the advertised position, I knew that I was qualified for this job. The receptionist greeted me warmly, made a call, and asked me to take a seat in the waiting area. All I could think about was money and how great it would be to work for a nationally recognized insurance chain. I saw many people coming and going as I sat there and waited. I realized that I would fit in quite comfortably here. Complete strangers were smiling at me as they walked by. Yes, this could be a real opportunity for me. I only had to wait for five minutes before an elderly woman exited the elevator and walked over to greet me. She shook my hand and told me she would be conducting the interview. We went up to the eighth floor and entered a very prestigious office. This office was indeed hers. I was hired within five minutes.

Miss Snaggletooth and Gee, What a Mistress

My cubicle was inside the fancy office, tucked away, back in a corner. Every single day, I arrived at work on time. This was not always easy to do with the new baby, an unreliable babysitter, and a car that only ran half the time. Yet, somehow, I managed to make it work on time every single day. I wanted so desperately to prove to myself and to the world that I could hold down a job and be a wife and a mother, all at the same time. I wasn't going to let anything get in my way and derail me.

Miss Snaggletooth had ideas of her own for me. She was about sixty years old, polished, and extremely professional looking. I could feel her dislike of me from the third week on. Here I was, showing up every day to work, twenty years young and beautiful, and wearing very fashionable clothes and designer look-alike heels that I purchased at "knock off" stores or made myself. I still managed to look professional, even though I was forty years her junior. But the deal breaker was that I could do twice as much work as she did in an hour. Miss Snaggletooth started piling on the work and quit doing any of her own. At first, I didn't even mind.

When I was told that I could no longer take lunch breaks, everything changed. My superior went to lunch daily with the president of the company and came back reeking of his cologne. Often, her lunch breaks lasted for three hours. Everyone in the company knew that she was his mistress, including his wife.

President's Office Next Door
and He Needs Me—What For?

As time went on, the president called me into his office frequently. In the beginning, it was for legitimate purposes. Very quickly, it became obvious that the president of this national organization wanted more from me than just secretarial services. One day, he asked if I would like to attend a golf excursion with him. I declined, telling him I had much work to do. He told me that my superior could handle it that afternoon. I walked back in to the office next door and told Miss Snaggle-tooth about the president's offer. She became enraged and forbid me to go on the golf outing.

I was relieved, because I had no plans of going. As I sat in my cubicle, I listened to my superior and the president of the company as they argued. The president came into my cubicle and told me that he was my boss and I had to do what I was told. He ordered me to wear golf clothes the following day to work. I responded that I could not comply. He asked me if I wanted a raise of a hundred and fifty dollars per paycheck to be his right-hand girl. I asked him exactly what my duties would be. The president simply said, "The same things your boss does." This meant a raise of three hundred dollars a month. Today, this would be like getting a raise of fifteen hundred dollars a month. I cannot begin to tell you how hard it was to turn this money down. But I did. The following day, Miss Snaggletooth went on a golf outing with the president.

The Big Blow Up—'She' Did Not Act Like a Lady

The day after the golf trip was pure hell for me. Miss Snaggle-tooth had not gotten over the president's offer to me. She knew that her years of being his mistress were soon to be replaced by a younger woman, even if it wasn't me. But for right now, her focus was on me. She wanted me out of that office and the earlier, the better.

I was given document after document to type, fax, and send out. The faster I completed one, the quicker she would give me another. It was almost as if I was in a race against time. As the end of the day approached, I was given a rather lengthy document to type. This was going to another president's office and there could be no errors. To terrorize me and sucker punch

43

me some more, Miss Snaggletooth chose to stand over me as I typed the document. Naturally, I couldn't get it right.

This was back in the day before there were computers. We used old fashioned typewriters with non-correcting keys. Mistakes were normally corrected with whiteout or special corrector tape. The only problem was that you could still see where the original mistake had been made. For this special document, no mistakes were allowed.

With Miss Snaggletooth hovering over me, I just could not get it right. I must have tried to type that document at least thirty times. Now, I ask you, who could have done any better under the same circumstances? I believe the answer is nobody. My hands were sweaty, I asked to get a drink and was refused, I asked to use the restroom and was refused. I finally looked up at her and asked if I could finish the document the next day. Quickly, she told me, "You are going to sit here until you get it done. I don't care how long it takes!"

Tears started flowing down my face as I looked at her. There was no sympathy as she stared at me. It was obvious she wanted me to fail and to fail miserably at this task. I told Miss Snaggletooth that I could not complete the task without a bathroom break. She laughed right in my face. Miss Professional wasn't acting very professional at all. I mean, she laughed so hard I thought she would pee her professional panties. I couldn't believe it. Here I was simply asking to use the bathroom and she was refusing me. How absurd! I had sat in that same chair for over three hours trying to type this same document with her hovering over me. This was insanity.

I decided at that moment that I wasn't going to let anyone treat me like that. I pushed my chair back, picked up my purse, gathered my family pictures from my desk, and announced that

I was going home. Miss Snaggletooth started screaming pro-fanities at me. She called me a young slut and a whore. She asked me if I realized how I flaunted myself around all the men, especially the president. She said that I needed the job, but I could never get another job like that one because she wouldn't give me a good recommendation. In a fit of rage, this crazy woman screamed at me, "Bitch, you're fired. Don't ever come back here!" I walked right past her and glared at her without saying a word.

"Bitch, you're fired!" Those are words that one likely never forgets. I don't care how they're said, when you hear the words, "You're fired!" it hurts.

Today the above scenario would never have gotten that far. I probably would have gotten up from my desk much earlier, gone into the bathroom, taken off my panties, dipped them in the toilet, and handed them to her as I walked out the door while telling her to shove it. Yes, if someone wants to call me a bitch, I might as well live up to the name!

Directed Journaling

❖ *At this very moment, I just realized that I was sucker punched by my husband when he left me just hours after delivering our first-born child. Have you ever felt sucker punched, but you didn't even realize it until later—like decades later? How would or how did you handle that?*

❖ *Do we let our jobs define us and if so, what can we do to change this? Men have always been more characterized by their jobs than women. Women are identified by their friendships and person-alities, instead of their jobs. How can we change the way society views us as individuals?*

❖ *Does the loss of a job change who we are on the "inside?" If you said "yes," please explain how that happens. Men, speak up!*

❖ *Getting sucker punched through job loss is gut-wrenching. Describe some of the best ways to pick yourself back up again and rise to the top after a job loss. How do/did you get back on top or are you still feeling sucker punched?*

❖ *What can we do for ourselves or to help our friends so the feelings of being sucker punched are never experienced again during job loss?*

CHAPTER

Mid-Life Crisis Can Feel Like Being Sucker Punched

"The morning of my thirtieth birthday, I ran into the bathroom and looked into the mirror. I was expecting to see a new, glamorous me. Instead, what I found in the bright lights, were crow's feet around my eyes staring back at me. I thought to myself instantly, 'Holy crap, you look old!' I wanted to cry. Big plans were on the table for that night. Nevertheless, I felt like they needed to be put on hold. I wasn't going to go anywhere looking like an old hag. Was this what I had to look forward to during my mid-life years? Surely I had at least another twenty years or more before this mid-life crap was going to hit me. I hadn't even reached my prime of life yet—you know, the one with all the great sex and everything! If this is what I had to look forward to, I didn't want to celebrate any more birthdays."

~ Dr. Gayle Joplin Hall.

Was That Thirtieth Birthday a Mid-Life Crisis?

My birthday was no crisis and by golly I earned those crow's feet. I'd worked hard for those, as well as the laugh lines around my lips. As I've aged, I've learned to be proud of the way I look. In fact, the older I've gotten, the more self-esteem I've gained. My thirtieth was a glorious time, shared with my husband and close friends. I was confident in my skin, with my body, and my presence.

Transitions were taking place in my life. I was enjoying my new advertising business and reaping the rewards. To show off my success, I bought and drove a brand new Cadillac with customized plates. I was so proud of myself. However, my husband had trouble with my newfound success. The Chamber of Commerce was my second home. You see, I was in charge of Membership Drives and the Speakers Bureau. I was so active in the community that almost everyone knew me. I loved my life. My husband would come home from weekly business trips and expect me to be home waiting for him. In other words, my world was supposed to stop the minute he walked through our front door. This was unsettling to me. I still had my own life, or did I?

Is Mid-Life Transition the Same as a Mid-Life Crisis?

Erik Erikson was one of the first psychologists to state that we continue to grow even as we go through different stages of life. He didn't say that we stop learning or growing once we finish adolescence. Erikson declared that from the ages of forty to sixty-five, we're ready to look to the future and be concerned about others. We have a need to feel productive for the benefit of society. Erikson says this is also known as generativity versus self absorption or stagnation.

What happens if a person doesn't feel productive, has no goals, or is left feeling stagnant, bitter, and unfulfilled? According to Daniel Levinson, people will live a life of decay and resignation if they don't go through a mid-life transition. In other words, a mid-life transition is normal for most of the population. However, according to McCrea and Costa, five percent of people will experience a mid-life crisis, which is painful and disruptive. In the absence of goal setting, this five percent will experience frustration. Therefore, it is relatively normal for many people to experience mid-life transitions, whereas a mid-life crisis is not normal.

These two mid-life "states" are not the same thing. I highly disagree with the percentages provided by the "experts" and believe approximately fifty percent of our population experiences a mid-life crisis at some point in their lives. Yes, we will see divorces, men running off with younger women, women running off with younger men (cougars—meow!), and broken homes, but does the crisis always have to be devastating?

Men and Women are Different—
So Are Our Mid-Life Crises

We are different creatures by nature. Men have always had to think about putting food on the table and supporting their families. When men lose their jobs, it is one of the worse sucker punches of all. It was their job to be the "head of the house." Think about the television shows from the fifties, such as *I Love Lucy* or *Leave it to Beaver*. Lucy didn't work outside the home and neither did June Cleaver. It was obvious who the breadwinners were. Very clear role models were recognized in the households.

When did that all change? I suppose the sixties revolution

had something to do with it. Women were burning their bras and demanding equal rights. During the seventies, women wanted it all. We wanted to stay home with our children if we felt like it, we wanted to break the glass ceiling at work if we felt like it, and we wanted to feel equal with our male counterparts. In the bedroom, we wanted to take charge and finally help him discover our "G" spots. Truly, we did want it all.

Ladies, let's admit it. If we can't figure out what we want at the moment, how can the men in our lives know what to do for us? Women have fought so hard to break into the corporate world that they expect more from their jobs. At the age of forty-five, if they're disenchanted, women are very likely to leave their jobs and start completely over. Often times, men do not have this opportunity. Additionally, women tend to look further down the road than men do. Studies have shown women are twice as likely as men to be hopeful about their future during mid-life. Women may first turn inward, go back to school, write a novel, or take action to help themselves. However, they have a tremendous urge to help others. I don't call this a crisis. This is merely a transition phase of mid-life

Warning Signals of a Crisis

There are several warning signals of a mid-life crisis. These are some of the basic ones, although they are not the same for everyone. If you notice your partner or yourself sinking into deep depression, this is definitely a sign of something going wrong. Please seek the help of a medical physician. Worrying about things more than before is another sign of a crisis. If your partner is unhappy all the time, complaining most of the time, overly tired for no reason, has a loss of sex drive, experiences extreme changes in eating habits, has feelings of being hopeless, is becoming withdrawn from society, and is anxious for no apparent reason, these are definitely warning signals of a potential mid-life crisis. The infamous crisis can happen whether you have a penis or a vagina. It crosses both gender lines.

The Men's Story

Men want to be valued at work and seem to gauge their self-respect based on how they're doing at their jobs. They want to feel respected and to be successful on the job. Yes, they may worry about losing some hair, getting flabby, and not looking as sexy as they used to. One day, they may wake up and realize that they're not twenty-five anymore. To make up for this during a crisis mode, men may seek younger women who value them. One hopes these men realize that over fifty percent of the time the younger women are chasing them only for their money. The new sports car, the expensive vacations, and a much younger woman are usually all it takes for men to feel relief from crisis mode. This is not to say that a mid-life crisis doesn't hurt, because it does. Seventy percent of the time, it is the woman who leaves the man and files for divorce (in the forty to seventy age group). Nothing feels quite like being sucker punched than when you get slapped with divorce papers. It is embarrassing and it hurts. It is a known fact that men are much happier when they are married.

Cowboy Boots and a Harley—Wait, Were These Moments of a Mid-Life Crisis?

Did I say something about cowboy boots and a Harley? Yes, I sure did and no, these were not moments of mid-life crisis. They were moments of sheer bliss! When I moved to Texas several years ago, I went dancing every weekend. The first time I went to a country western bar, I asked why people were moving around and around like on pony rides. I'd never seen country dancing before nor heard that kind of music. My genre was hip-hop and R&B. I had great fun learning new dances with new partners every weekend. I was in my early forties and danced with men as young as eighteen and as old as forty. The usual age of my dance partner ended up being around twenty-eight.

During my forties, I went on my very first cruise with my sister and mother. It was more fun than I dreamed possible. Since then, I've cruised on at least fifteen more adventures. I've jumped out of an airplane and parachuted, survived living in sub-zero temperatures, kayaked with a good friend in the Cayman Islands, danced under the stars with a sexy cruise ship photographer all night long, and joined a motorcycle group. I was a patched member of Bikers Against Child Abuse (BACA) for two years as the only female Harley rider. I was not the "bitch on the back." I also graduated with my Masters degree in administration. All these were accomplished during my forties. Now, if this sounds like a crisis, then I guess I had plenty. But really folks, none of these were a crisis. They were adventures in life that I wanted to explore. There's so much more I can add to the list, but I won't bore you.

Tick Tock Goes Our Clock

You see, the difference between men and women is that women are constantly reminded of time. Our biological clocks are ticking. Hence, we're ever aware of the passing time. We can change our minds as often as we'd like to and we do. But that clock is always ticking. Women's turmoil is due to multi-tasking, issues in our personal lives, and stress associated with trying to break the glass ceiling. It's no wonder that some of us are sucker punched, suffer breakdowns, and have a mid-life crisis or two. Quite often, a crisis can be the sunshine to brighter tomorrows if we open our eyes and just bust through the crap that is dragging us down.

Directed Journaling

❖ Did you know there was a difference between a mid-life crisis and something normal, such as a mid-life transition? How have you handled your transitions in life up to this point?

❖ Have the "methods" you've followed worked for you? Why or why not?

❖ Do men and women suffer mid-life crises differently and if so, please explain. Is there a right way or a wrong way to handle the crisis so it does not feel like you're getting sucker punched?

❖ Does a mid-life crisis automatically equal the feelings of getting sucker punched? Why or why not? Does it always have to end up badly when there's a crisis?

❖ What advice would you give, if you've passed the mid-life transition phase, to others to help them avoid their transition from turning into a crisis and a potential sucker punch?

6
CHAPTER

The Sinful Sucker Punch—A Nervous Breakdown; the Outcome, a Doctor—*Me!*

"Throughout my entire life, I've completed projects ahead of time. My Type A personality has pushed me to excel and be the best at everything I've ever tried to do. This was instilled in me as a very young child. Producing less than the best was not acceptable in our home. I grew up with the same expectations of myself, which worked well for me until I decided to get my advanced degree in psychology with my PhD."

~ Dr. Gayle Joplin Hall.

Guts, Law Books, or Brains

In 2005, I lost my job, was scared silly, and didn't know where the future would lead me. For the past nine years I'd been a single mother raising my teenage son. Many decisions had to be made the minute I was fired that week before Christmas. I considered going to medical school like my brother had. Psychiatry didn't interest me as I didn't want to limit myself to just talking with crazy people all day long. The field of gynecology and obstetrics really piqued my interest until I thought about the second year of medical school when I would have to work with cadavers. There was no way I'd get through that, or the smell. Very quickly I put that thought to rest.

I'd considered going to law school when living in North Dakota during which time my education would all have been paid for and I would now be in private practice. In my heart, I knew this what I truly wanted to do. As a lawyer, I'd work pro bono with domestic violence victims. I also knew that a financially secure income would not be achievable if I lived my dream of helping people that way. It would be satisfying, but how would I support my son and myself?

Once my house sold in May of 2006, I moved to Dallas, leased a new home (deciding to keep the stash from the sale of my house), and began investigating options for going to post graduate school. Psychology intrigued me, so there was no question of what I was going to study. I wanted to guide and coach people into making good decisions for themselves (and am doing just that with my business, www.DrHallonCall.com). I wanted to teach college classes, engage as a professional empowerment speaker, and write books. I was called to help more people on a broader scale and could do just that by earning my doctorate in Psychology. When I finally selected my school, the advisors told me to expect a minimum of four through seven years to complete my field of practice. I immediately replied, "I'll be finished before four years has passed." And I did complete everything ahead of schedule.

Brains it Was

Never in my wildest dreams did I realize what I'd signed up for. One class was equal to five credit hours at the doctoral level. Each candidate was advised to never take more than two classes per ten-week-quarter session. This meant ten credit hours in ten weeks. Understand, this was a lot of studying and tons of reading. Additionally, two written papers were required each week. This was clearly my full-time job. I didn't even try to find work outside of my home during the first three months of school. Thinking I could handle more classes than the average student, I signed up for three post graduate classes at the same time. Those fifteen hours felt like forty-five. Good God, what was I thinking?

I slept an average of four hours a night for the next ten weeks. All I could think about was, "I had to get A's in all three classes." It drove me crazy. Somehow, I managed to get my A's and promised myself to never again take three classes at the same time. I learned my lesson. For the rest of my post graduate education, I took only two classes for ten credit hours a session.

Limits Were Quickly Learned

My life was based around school, what was due, and when it was due. Everything else was secondary, and I do mean everything. Being a student at the post graduate level at my age was not easy. I needed complete quiet and solitude or I couldn't study. In every single class I became the leader. In 2007, I had an upcoming surgery scheduled. I was so fearful of falling behind, that I completed two, twenty-page papers for two concurrent classes six weeks ahead of time. I received A's on both of them. As I look back now, I think how crazy I was to have done that!

Advanced Inferential Statistics was the class that had me frightened the most. I put it off until the very end, right before my comprehensive exams. So many of my peers had talked about how dreadful it was, how they had failed and had to repeat the course, and how horrible running the software was, plus trying to figure out the results—I just knew I was doomed. I was so knotted up inside with fear that I felt sucker punched every time I thought about that class. I became physically ill just thinking about it. As it turned out, I became the leader of this class and could now teach people how to read SPSS software results.

Comprehensive Exam and Assignment of My Department Mentor

After completing all the classes at the doctoral level, students must take comprehensive exams. These are given to assess critical learning skills and knowledge. Although I fretted about taking the exam (because I worried about everything), what really had me upset was the lack of communication between me and my department mentor. I listened as the other students discussed conversations they had with their mentors and wondered why my mentor never sent e-mails or called me. I sent my mentor an e-mail asking why he hadn't communicated with me. He responded that it wasn't necessary. I was dumbfounded.

I was leaving on a family vacation, so I took my comprehensive exam early. Both my advisor and my mentor had suggested that I wait to take the exam until after my vacation. On the third day of our family cruise at sea, I received the news. I passed my exams with flying colors. With no support from my advisor or my mentor, I kicked it!

Fired My Adviser but Had Other Plans for My Mentor

The next two years were living hell for me. I fired the advisor who wouldn't support me with my decision about the comprehensive exam. I had the next advisor for the remainder of my two years while earning my doctorate. She was awesome and helpful.

My mentor absolutely hated my guts and felt it was his duty in life to punish me. He made me redo papers repeatedly. Then he'd hold onto them as long as he could before returning them with his comments. When I questioned his comments or pointed out that he was wrong, all the while ignoring his numerous spelling and grammatical errors, he became enraged. There were too many delays on his part to count. My peers, who had started the exams with me and failed exams, were now surpassing me because they didn't have to repeat their work six to nine times. I asked a different mentor for help and even spoke with him on the phone. He told me my current mentor had a "swollen ego that needed to be constantly fed." All conversations were documented and stored on permanent electronic files.

You may be wondering why I didn't fire my mentor. Everyone advised me to fire him. He was not allowed to fire me, but I could fire him. I made a simple decision that, since he was ruining my life, I'd make him suffer right along with me throughout my dissertation phase.

Very quickly, I realized this was a money-maker for the

school. As long as they had me in their system so that I could not graduate, they were raking in the dough. My post graduate education cost me $105,000. If my mentor hadn't played those games, it would have cost around $65,000.

Preparation for a Dissertation Equals Gobs of Work

For years leading up to this point, I knew what my dissertation was going to be. I'd even talked about this with my mentor at colloquia sessions, face-to-face, prior to starting this phase of my education. He told me it was a great idea. My qualitative inquiry was going to be private interviews with battered women who were not living in shelters. The focus was going to be on resiliency and successful women. The idea had been planted in my head by another senior Doctor whom I respected very much. He said, "Write your dissertation about women like you." So, that was the plan.

Before students begin their dissertations, they are required to turn in a qualifications sheet, their resume, and write a summary of what their expected outcome is. They also must write their goal expectations and why they feel they are qualified to conduct their study. This is sent to the mentor before anything else and is signed off on. My mentor knew well in advance what my qualifications were.

For seven months, the Methodology Review Forms (MRF) were sent back and forth to my mentor as I was being led in the direction of writing the title and basic information for my qualitative study. I had my paper half-written, although it is true that I did not know how to write at the doctoral level, other than the thousands of pages I had read. I had not begun to conduct research, obviously. There are *many* steps before that. This may not sound like much, so let me put it in perspective.

I'd read over two hundred complete dissertations (some with five hundred-plus pages), researched and studied three hundred and fifty Journal Articles, and devoured book after book in the areas of resiliency, battered women's syndrome, PTSD, and pioneers in the field of domestic violence. Additionally, I had logged over five thousand hours of volunteer work. Furthermore, I had been a victim of domestic violence myself and had been free from the situation for over fifteen years. I believed this made me exceptionally qualified to conduct my inquiry.

A Nervous Breakdown is So Easy

One day as I was working at the computer, I received an unexpected e-mail from the department head, someone I had never spoken to. This e-mail message was brief and stated simply, "You are not qualified to conduct this study. Choose another subject." I read the message again, hoping I'd misread it. Was this some kind of sick joke? "What do you mean I'm not qualified to conduct this study?" I screamed out loud. My youngest son was standing behind me in my little study room when the message came across my computer. He saw me freak out. He heard me scream. He watched me as I cried. He observed my trembling, the mortified look on my face, and the snot flying everywhere. He watched me as I collapsed in a heap on the floor. I was sucker punched right smack in the gut. My baby son was eighteen and he was frightened. This wasn't his mom who always had everything under control, right? I asked him to leave my room. I found out later that he called his own dad, whom he rarely spoke to, and made a couple of other calls, as well.

What a Nervous Breakdown Felt Like

There I lay, in a pile of tears in the middle of my floor. I couldn't stop crying, sobbing, and swearing. Why did I deserve to have my title rejected after all this work? I knew in my heart that I was qualified and I also knew this was my mentor's way of getting back at me for challenging him so many times. I didn't know what to do, but I knew that I needed help—and very quickly, as I felt my life crumbling to pieces. This humbled me in a way I will never be able to describe any better than this. It was humiliating, pure torture, and I felt a death inside of me because my dream had been put into a grave. It became apparent very quickly that I would be starting completely over from scratch. I was mortified.

I Need to See A Shrink?

I managed to call a dear friend in the medical industry and tell her what happened. She had no idea what working on a dissertation was like, but she did know that I was never available to have any fun because I was always reading. It took me two days and many phone calls to arrange to see the best psychiatrist in all of Dallas.

As I sat in the foyer waiting for my turn to see the psychiatrist, I wondered what the meeting would be like. So much was running through my head. I thought only crazy people went to shrinks. Was I crazy and insane just because I had a nervous breakdown? The doctor came in, shook my hand, and sat at his desk. Prior to my arrival, I had filled out a twenty-three page intake document and faxed it to the doctor's office. The doctor picked up my intake forms, briefly looked through them, and laid them down the desk beside him. My initial thought was,

"Great. He hasn't even looked at the damn papers after all the work I went through filling them out."

He proved me wrong. I was with the doctor for over three hours, uninterrupted. He knew every detail about me from the intake document. Not only had he read my information prior to my arrival, he had studied it. This was the most thorough and comprehensive visit I've ever had with any doctor. After the doctor determined that I wasn't going to kill myself, he prescribed anti-anxiety and anti-depressant medication and scheduled an appointment the following week. I saw the doctor weekly for three months, biweekly for six months, and monthly for another six months. He truly saved my life in more ways than one.

Singing "I'm a Nut Bag" To the World

For the first time in my entire life, I realized that I was not super woman. I couldn't do everything I wanted to do while trying to complete my doctorate. I couldn't take care of the thirty-two hundred square foot house. I couldn't take care of rose gardens and newly planted trees outside. I couldn't buy groceries, cook meals, and be everything to everyone all the time. When my youngest son saw me fall on the floor in a crying heap of tears, it was the first time in his life that he realized I was just normal, like him. Through self-therapy, I realized that my son never thought he could meet up to my superior expectations. Since I had such high standards for myself, he thought I expected the same of him. Although this was not true, it took me having a nervous breakdown to allow him to see that I was just a normal person.

Working as a college professor during the last three years of my doctoral studies, it became apparent to me that I should disclose some of my personal trials and tribulations to my students. This was one way for them to learn that if I could be beaten down and sucker punched over and over again, and still manage to rise back up to the top, they could also. My students often asked about my progress and when I completed my doctorate, all of my classes threw parties in my honor. I was loved by most of my students. Many of them remain in touch with me still today and I love them all dearly.

The Last Minute and Still No Clue

Here I was at the end of all sixteen milestones required to graduate with my doctorate degree. I had sent several e-mails to my mentor asking if I was on the list for graduation. He simply never responded. Thankfully, my advisor sent me the fantastic news that after four miserable years of work on my doctorate, I would be graduating. Never again would anyone be able to tell me that I wasn't qualified to conduct a study. I always loved research and I still do. I did not let him strip that from me.

Call Me Doctor Gayle Hall

In 2010, my dissertation was published. When I went to commencement in New Orleans, I fanaticized that my mentor would be there so I could walk over to him and say, "And you can call me Dr. Hall." However, he was not there to ruin my momentous day as I walked that stage. I made it in spite of him and I am darn proud of myself. Hooray!

Directed Journaling

❖ *When you've had to make a major life decision, how did you go about choosing what to do? What was the biggest guiding factor? Think really hard.*

❖ If faced with no support from your school, employer, or family, how would you handle major stress with changes in any of those areas? If you are past this stage of life and in the "golden years" how do you handle major changes now?

❖ If you felt a nervous breakdown coming, or even if you felt extreme anxiety, would you take the proper steps to seek medical help? Why or why not? Would you be afraid of being judged by others who are close to you? If they sucker punched you for seeking help, how would you handle that?

❖ Who is your biggest personal support system and why? If you have nobody to turn to, where are some places with people who might be able to help you? Are you aware that there are hospitals in almost every city that cannot turn away patients who can't pay their bills? Do you know there are outreach centers in almost every major city to help with mental health needs and stress?

❖ If you were sucker punched for admitting a nervous breakdown to your family members and needed medication, how would you handle that? You must learn to stick up for yourself and I'll show you how to do that later on in this book.

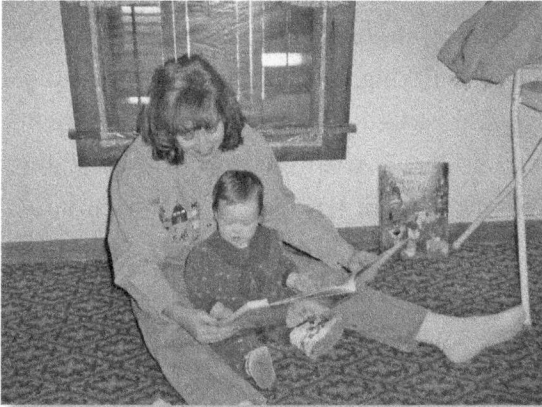

CHAPTER

7

Duped—Can You Call This Being Sucker Punched? Hell, Yes!

"Ever since I was eight years old, I've dreamed of being a grandmother. Now, I realize this sounds a little silly, but I wanted to be the grandmother who rocks her grandbaby to sleep, who keeps the baby for the weekend, and is an active part of her grandbaby's life. I wanted to live next door to my grandbaby, to read books to my grandbaby, and to pass down knowledge and family history to my grandbaby. I don't know why, but I always figured I would have a grandbaby in my mid-forties. And the birth—I would witness the birth of my first grandbaby. I had it all figured out so I could be the perfect grandmother. This was important to me. But then, what do eight-year-old girls know anyway?"

~ Dr. Gayle Joplin Hall.

New Year's Surprise

It was New Year's Eve and we'd just finished playing a game of Scrabble. My oldest child, who was nineteen at the time, looked at me from across the room and announced, "Mom, I've got a surprise. I don't know how you're going to react, so I've put off telling you." A thousand things ran through my mind. Was this child of mine going to tell me he was dropping out of school, that he was gay, or that he'd gotten married? Those were my immediate thoughts and none of them would have set me on fire. I was completely unprepared for what he was about to say. He was smirking, and the sibling who also had kept the secret from me was equally enjoying the moment. I begged, "Please just tell me. You know you can tell me anything." My son looked at me from ten feet away and declared, "I have a daughter and she looks just like you." I asked him to repeat what he'd just said. Surely I'd heard this incorrectly. Then he said it again, very mischievously. "Yeah mom, I have a baby girl and she is eleven months old." I couldn't move, think, or speak for a couple of seconds. I was numb. I had just received one of the lowest blows, a gigantic sucker punch from my own child.

Surprises Suck—Happy New Year!

I've never liked surprises in my entire life and this one took the cake. My immediate reaction after getting over the initial shock was simply, "Where is she?" "Who is she?" "Tell me about her." "What's her name?" I wanted to know every detail about this baby. After all, she was my first grandchild. My son walked over to me, handed me a picture, and said, "This is Hope. Her name is Hope Elena Dylan." Still completely freaked out, I asked where she lived. I was merely told, "In Ohio." I wanted details, explicit details. My son explained very little, except to say his father had told him the baby should be aborted. When my son had gotten a young girl pregnant (the one I'd met at his high school graduation) the advice he received from his father was to pay for an abortion. I knew nothing of the situation.

Still in shock, I begged for more information about Hope. Where were the grandparents? How could I see this grandbaby of mine—the one I didn't even know existed? My son refused to answer my questions. Furthermore, he seemed amused as I cried, sobbed, and pleaded for more information about Hope. The only thing I knew was her grandmother and grandfather's name, as well as her mother's name and that they lived in rural Ohio, somewhere near the high school my son had graduated from. I realized, and verbalized out loud, that for nineteen months—nineteen months—I'd been kept in complete darkness about this baby. I'd missed out on the entire pregnancy, the birth of my first grandchild, and the first eleven months of her life. I was sucker punched and it almost killed me because the emotional pain was so intense.

Fleeing, Rather than Facing the Grandparents' Reaction

I told my teen he was going to have to tell his grandparents about the situation. We'd all gathered for New Year's Eve in Missouri at my parents' home. He told me he wasn't about to explain Hope to his grandparents. He was afraid to own up to what he'd done and how he'd handled the situation. Both he and his sibling tried to leave in the middle of the night. However, they were unable to as my son had locked the car keys in the trunk of the car. He had to wait until morning to leave. Yes, karma bites one in the butt every time.

A Picture of Me—The Grandbaby I Never Knew Existed

Clinging to the picture of Hope, all I could think of was finding her. Here was this little angel who was the very picture of me when I was a baby. Furthermore, she looked just like her father, my son, when he was a baby. Hope was so beautiful. I was obsessed with locating her. For the next two days while I was at my parents' house, I called at least three hundred telephone numbers seeking the grandparents. A couple of times, I thought I had found the baby, only to be disappointed when I asked for the mother by name. Finally, after tedious work, I hit the jackpot!

A woman answered the phone and when I asked for the mother by name, I discovered I had the right home. The woman on the other side of the line was apprehensive of me. She asked me many questions. Naturally, she was hesitant to believe who I was and why I wanted to know Hope. Why, after almost two years, did I now show interest in this baby girl? If I was the paternal grandmother, how could I not be aware of all that had happened during the first nineteen months since pregnancy? I could not blame her one bit. If I'd been in her shoes, I would have been relentless in my questioning of me. Hope's maternal grandmother and grandfather hated my son and his father for wanting to abort the baby. I can't say that I fault them. My job was to convince them that I'd known nothing, absolutely nothing, the entire time.

Begging for Forgiveness and One Chance

Never in my entire life did I beg so hard for forgiveness for another person like I did for my son. The baby's family wanted nothing to do with my son or his father. They associated me with them, of course, even though I'd been divorced. I never would have chosen abortion for any grandbaby of mine. I begged and pleaded for forgiveness for my son and then I asked what I could do to make it right. The only thing I could think of was trying to see this baby, this first grandbaby, in person. I wanted to hold her. I wanted to touch her face. I wanted to hear her babble. I wanted her to know that I loved her. Finally, after long conversations numerous times during the following week, the grandparents of this baby allowed me to see Hope. My heart was overjoyed and skipped beats. I booked my flight the next day and within one week of learning about Hope, I was on a jet from North Dakota to Ohio to see my first grandchild.

Meeting Hope's Family

Apprehension and sheer trepidation were my feelings as I knocked on the door at Hope's grandparents' home. When I arrived would I to be sucker punched again? What if I got there and they wouldn't allow me to see the baby because they didn't like me or had changed their minds? With these thoughts running through my psyche, I was quickly reminded again of how worry strips us of time. I was welcomed with open arms. As I walked in the door, I saw her. My grandbaby, the one I'd dreamed of since I was a little girl, was sitting on the floor playing.

My hands were full of presents that happened to be mostly books. Without asking, I took off my coat and immediately sat down on the floor with the gifts. Hope came over to me and started tearing in to the treasures. She was so beautiful, perfect in every way, and truly was a miniature "me." I was a bit freaked out, but in a good way. Hope opened present after present. I sat on the floor and read book after book with Hope in my lap. My visit lasted for three days. For the rest of my life, I will always remember those three days and the meeting of my first grand-baby.

Cards, Letters, and Visits

For the next several years, I went to visit Hope on a regular basis. Her grandmother liked me so much that I was invited to stay overnight in their home during my visits. I took Hope shopping and the funny thing is, she loves shoes as much as I do. Even as a little girl, she loved shoes. I watched Hope swim and play with her friends, watched her play softball, and witnessed her mastering baton. Throughout the years, Hope would send me letters and cards. I know I don't need to mention that I've kept them all. They're priceless to me, just as she is.

Hope asked me about her father sometimes in letters and during our visits. She would say, "Why doesn't my dad care about me?" and "Why doesn't my dad want to know me?" or "Won't you please talk to my dad and ask him if he will see me?" Little did she know that I had tried on more than one occasion to speak with my son. He told me to never bring up the subject of Hope again because it caused problems for my son with his wife. And so, I played that game with my son for sixteen years. Then, I decided no more games.

The Big Dallas

The last time Hope came to visit me, she was sixteen years old. She had never been to a big city like Dallas before. I was so excited that she wanted to come see me and spend time with me. This was a dream come true. I pampered her just like a sixteen-year-old girl ought to be pampered. After our pedicure, we went shopping. Then we shopped more and even more. The most special moment for me was when we sat in my office and just talked. Hope talked about her boyfriend, her plans for the future, and life. She is beautiful beyond words. Hope is brilliant, gorgeous, talented, unique, and more exceptional than words can express. I'm so blessed that we had that extraordinary time together.

Intentional Lost Time

Out of nowhere, some of my son's family members are now interested in Hope's life. This has caused confusion, disruption and pain for Hope. Naturally, she has wondered why after sixteen years, they are now curious about her life. Where were they all those previous years? Where were they all those other birthdays and holidays when they were celebrating the rest of their families' special days? Why was she forgotten and put on the back burner to sizzle away? After the initial contact with her birth father, my son, she was forgotten about again during Christmas and her birthday. Yes, it's true. Hope can be shoved to the back burner at any time by people who do not truly care about her or love her as she deserves. A token gift here and there during the past year from those who do not even really know Hope—is that love? You tell me. Thankfully, Hope understands how much I've loved her since the moment I discovered her existence in the world.

Sucker Punched Children

Hope is one of many sucker punched children in the world. I can't begin to think what it would feel like to have a parent who doesn't love you or who doesn't even acknowledge your existence. That must be hell and feel unimaginably awful. Think what this does to a child's self esteem. The child is asking why he or she isn't good enough to deserve love. This same child grows up feeling unworthy of love. Due to choices made for the child early in his or her life, the outcome is a self-fulfilling prophecy of "not being good enough" for many years. Truly, this makes me sick to my stomach. No child, or any person for that matter, deserves to feel "not good enough."

Directed Journaling

❖ *If a family member kept a secret from you and then announced it as a "surprise" that knocked the crap out of you, do you think this might feel like a sucker punch? When have you been sucker punched by a family member? Provide all the details.*

❖ *Why do you think it hurts so much when a family member or very close friend delivers a blow that knocks you down? Do you have any idea how to avoid sucker punches right now?*

❖ *Do you believe we have unrealistic expectations from our family members and/or close friends and that is why we get sucker punched? Please explain.*

❖ *It is a proven fact that children with low self esteem do less than average compared with their peers in school, in general. How does one explain a child who can overcome this, such as Hope, in excelling with grades and all projects she managed to undertake?*

❖ *How would you have handled the news I received on New Year's— that of a baby who was almost one year old—your first grandbaby? Would you be angry, glad to know the news, upset about the surprise, or would you feel duped big time and sad about missing the birth of your first grandbaby and the first year of her life? What would you have done differently than what I did? How would you overcome that horrendous sucker punch to the belly?*

8

Are You Exempt From Being Sucker Punched? The Answer is "No." Learn To Avoid the Pitfalls of the Nasty Sucker Punched Syndrome™ (SPS)

"I've explained my early years of being bullied as a child, dishing out sucker punches as well as receiving some during dating and relationships, domestic violence, job loss, midlife crisis, and being duped. So many stories under each chapter could be told, but I'm waiting to hear your story. We've all been sucker punched at some point during our lives. How was I able to get back up after being knocked down time and again? How was I able to endure being sucker punched repeatedly? It is no secret. Anyone, at any time, can be sucker punched unless you learn how to avoid the oncoming blow. Self efficacy, otherwise known as a person's belief in his or her own competence, saved me throughout my adult years. Combined with optimism and resiliency, there was no way I would stay sucker punched for very long during the moment of crisis. I knew that I would persevere."

~ Dr. Gayle Joplin Hall.

Definition of the Sucker Punched Syndrome™ (SPS)

A syndrome is a group of signs and symptoms that, when combined together, is distinctive of a specific condition. This condition can be described as the disturbance in mental health or functions. In other words, this becomes a dysfunction. Neither this syndrome, nor the symptoms in this case, have anything to do with disease.

Symptoms of the Sucker Punched Syndrome™ (SPS) may include feelings of hopelessness, interpersonal distress, learned helplessness, a lack of self efficacy, having a pessimistic attitude, low self-esteem, expectations of repeated occurrences of abuse, and a high need for social approval.

Research and Inquiries

As a research scientist, I've developed a specific, quantifiable hypothesis that can be tested empirically. Throughout the years, when working with people and helping them overcome their fears, I noticed similar symptoms in people who had been knocked down. At the time, I hadn't named the syndrome yet. With over five thousand people in my studies, I've integrated evidence across time and place. I've acquired a consistent and precise understanding of human nature during this process. I've scientifically researched literature, as well as formed and tested my own hypothesis regarding the Sucker Punched Syndrome™ (SPS).

Hypothesis, Method, and Theory

An explicit, testable prediction was based on observation from the past twenty years. The population consisted of children as young as two years of age to adults as old as ninety-eight. The hypothesis was, "People who are faced with negative circumstances repeatedly will expect negative situations again in the future." The conceptual variables were feelings of hopelessness, interpersonal distress, learned helplessness, a lack of self efficacy, pessimism, low self-esteem, and expectations of repeated occurrences of abuse.

Data was collected through self-report measures, observation, direct questions and answers, plus qualitative interviews while performing service work at the YWCA, Domestic Violence Agencies, United Way Agencies, Smart Street, BACA, Hospice, Homeless Shelters, The Salvation Army, Young Women's Civic Club, and Chamber of Commerce. Additionally, as a professor, I observed firsthand, many of my students doing a hundred eighty degree turnaround in their lives after attending my classes.

A theory was formed regarding why people behave the way they do. Specifically, the theory of the Sucker Punched Syndrome™ encompasses two or more of the symptoms (see the first paragraph in this chapter). This theory can be tested and is, therefore, reliable and valid. Both basic and applied research was used to assess the outcome.

Nature Versus Nurture

The nature versus nurture debate has been around for centuries. Each of us is born with certain vulnerabilities, such as a difficult temperament. Likewise, each of us is born with some protective factors, such as a high intelligence or an even-tempered personality that tend to increase resilience. These are genetic; otherwise known as nature. Throughout childhood and adolescence, variables in the environment can have different affects on our vulnerabilities and protective factors. Therefore, the same environment may produce dissimilar effects on different individuals. This is known as nurture in the great debate.

For example, a red haired girl who was bullied as a child may turn out to be a bully herself. On the other hand, another little red haired girl may turn out to be highly empathetic.

Bullying is the Biggest Killer in Middle School

For all of the parents who are reading this right now, bullying in grades five through nine is the biggest killer. This is a real phenomenon that needs to be taken seriously. When your child comes to you and tells you that he or she is the target of bullying, you need to take immediate precautions to protect your child. Many schools now have incorporated a zero tolerance for bullying. However, the proper officials must be notified of the issue at hand. Make this your first priority for your child or teen.

To Hell With Sticks and Stones

"Sticks and stones may break my bones, but words will never hurt me." Whoever coined this phrase obviously was never bullied or sucker punched. Well isn't that nice? Piercing, nasty words last a lifetime. Believe me, I know. So how did I manage to rise to the top after years of torture as a child and as an adult in an abusive marriage? Fortunately, I come from great genes and I am able to bounce back when I am knocked down. It hasn't always been this way. I have only mastered this during the past five years.

Anyone Can Be Sucker Punched

Anyone, at any time or place, can be sucker punched. One sneaky blow from the backside when you least expect it could knock you to your knees. Does this mean you should have your guard up at all times? No, but as we grow older and wiser, we learn who we can trust and who to let into our inner circle. These are usually our close friends or trusted family members. Everyone else is merely an acquaintance. People confuse friends with acquaintances. I see this happening every single day. To confuse the two is a huge mistake.

How to Avoid Being Sucker Punched

The first step to avoid being sucker punched is to surround yourself with like-minded people. This means that if you want to be positive, you associate with positive, up-beat people. Practice using positive psychology. If you think about things in a positive way, it will help. Positive and optimistic behavior go hand-in-hand. Stay away from naysayers who want to drag you down. Misery loves company and always has. Let's face it. The more you're around encouraging, optimistic people, the happier you'll be.

Avoid those who are constantly whining, full of drama, or who want to drag you into their mess. You did not make their mess and it is not your job to clean it up, either. When a red flag goes up, put your running shoes on and head for the hills. Sometimes this is not easy to do, especially if a family member is involved. Don't enable others, and stay out of the poop pile. I never said this would be easy. But what I can assure is that you will dodge the sucker punches before they ever fly your way if you learn to evade negativity.

Talk to people who have been in your shoes and ask them how they found their way out. Experience and wisdom speak volumes. How many times have we seen people make the same mistakes over and over again? Don't fall into this category. A mistake is a mistake when it happens once, you learn from it, and don't repeat it. On the other hand, if you make a mistake and then allow yourself to keep making that same mistake, this becomes a habit. Don't do that!

Practice the Law of Attraction. Simply stated, this means that what you put out into the universe is what you receive back in return. If you do good deeds, excellent things will come into your life. If you believe in good things, good things come your way. If you believe you are going to fail, if you are afraid, if you feel there is no way out of your situation (such as learned helplessness), that is exactly what you're going to get. Change is often scary. If you put garbage in, you will only be able to take garbage out. Be willing to take a step toward the trash can and dump being sucker punched ever again.

If You Do Get Slammed

Seek advice from a qualified lifestyle coach, counselor, or therapist who will work with you and help to restore your self esteem, self worth, and general outlook on life. It's difficult to be happy if you've been sucker punched repeatedly. Until you learn to value yourself as a person, you won't be able to experience fulfillment in daily activities. You may need to seek the help of a psychotherapist for free association to get past the old crap, or visit with a psychiatrist if medication is deemed necessary.

Directed Journaling

❖ *Have you ever felt hopeless to the point of giving up? How did you pull yourself out of that feeling at the time? How would you help a friend reduce the feeling of being sucker punched and hopeless?*

❖ *When was the last time you had interpersonal distress? What about the time before that? How did you handle it? Be precise.*

How would focusing on positive psychology and a positive outlook help you?

❖ *Seligman stated we may get depression from learned helplessness, the feeling that we have no control over our expected or important outcomes. Victims often experience learned helplessness. What would you do if you were experiencing learned helplessness? Could you break free and gain control or would you be like most people and surrender? How do you know what you might do? Give details.*

❖ *On a scale of 1 to 10, with 10 being the highest or best, where would you rate your own level of self esteem right now? What do you attribute this to?*

❖ *Are you going to implement any of the suggestions in this chapter to avoid being sucker punched in the future, such as shunning negative people, even if this means staying away from some of your own family members? Why or why not? Do you see the importance of the Law of Attraction and how this works? Please explain.*

CHAPTER 9

Optimism and Resiliency

"I am the eternal optimist. Since being a teenager, I've always looked on the bright side and believed good things would happen. I believed that love would find me if somehow I missed it along the way. I dreamed of having a close-knit family, dedicated friends, and a loving husband. I was optimistic about my life as it would unfold when I grew old. Would I be able to accomplish everything I had envisioned? Would my family continue to love me if I disappointed them or made mistakes? Would I be well-respected in my field of work? Would I have contributed somehow to society and have made it a better place? With each of those questions, the answer was most always 'Yes.' "

~ Dr. Gayle Joplin Hall.

Weathering the Storms

I have been asked numerous times how I managed to get through my difficult situations. Each and every time, I referred back to my world view on a generalized tendency to expect positive outcomes, otherwise known as optimism. Seligman states that an optimist will blame failure on factors that are temporary and external. Furthermore, this same optimistic person will credit success to aspects that are internal and permanent.

When I was being bullied as a little girl, I always wondered to myself why I was hated so much for being different. I realize that I looked different on the outside, but on the inside, I was just "me"—a normal little girl who loved playing with dolls, climbing trees, and dreaming of the day I could wear makeup, be a mother, and help people. Those who tortured me had no clue about who I really was.

The Difference Between Optimism and Pessimism

The distinction between an optimist and a pessimist is as different as night and day. A pessimistic person sees a glass as half full, believes that failures are internal and permanent, and expects bad things to happen. As the saying goes in Murphy's Law, if something can go wrong, it will go wrong. A pessimistic attitude reduces the chances of having rewarding relationships, a healthy lifestyle, and securing decent employment.

Research shows that optimists are generally healthier and have a stronger immune response to stress than pessimists do. Longitudinal studies have shown that over a fifty-year global span, optimists were less likely to have died in accidental, reckless, or violent deaths.

Social Perception—Was I Always a Freak?

When we meet people for the first time, we begin forming impressions about them immediately. Naturally, we notice the obvious attributes first. This is called Impression Formation. Physical attraction, combined with race, age, and the way one is dressed, make up the critical first impressions. Once formed, it is nearly impossible to erase that initial framework. Social psychologists may say this begins during childhood, but I will take it one step further. What is the first thing the labor and delivery nurse is looking for in the birthing room at the hospital? We are identified by our gender and labeled from the moment we are born, according to whether we have a penis or a vagina.

I was a hippie love child during my late teen years, and due to situational attributions, I changed to a professional career in my twenties through early forties. In other words, I had to change the way I looked due to my work environment. As I aged and became comfortable with myself, dispositional attributions kicked in and I was able to be the "real" me again, even as a college professor. During my years of teaching college psychology, I wore whatever I felt like and most of the time, I looked like my students. I had the pleasure of dressing just like I did when I was seventeen as a hippie love child in adoration of my namesake, Janis Joplin. Yes, I could wear designer suits and heels. But I could also dress down in my hat, boots, jeans, and love clothes. I guess I've always been a bit of a freak. And I must say, I love being my own person.

Resiliency is My Touchstone

By now you may be asking yourself how I was able to pick myself up after being punched down time and time again. In the first chapter, I explained the misery of being sucker punched as a child. Nevertheless, I was still able to get up every morning and go back to face those bullies. Resiliency had something to do with this. Resiliency, in the simplest form, means the ability to bounce back after suffering devastating blows in unsupportive or harmful environments. Because of my hardships, I developed resiliency. As a result of becoming resilient, I built up a trait called hardiness. Although I endured plenty of hits, my hardy personality supported me throughout the journey.

Do It To Me One More Time

Hardiness has three qualities: Commitment, Control, and Challenge (the three C's). Even though I was an easy target for the bullies when I was a child, I was committed to getting good grades. This was expected of me at home and I focused my attention on that. The control I *did* have was at home, bossing around my younger brother and sister. As a child, I challenged my mother to discover the new scabs all over my legs and arms that were a result of my nervousness from the bullying at school. Every single one of my sucker punches as a child made me stronger, more resilient, and developed my hardy personality so that I could handle what I was going to encounter in my adulthood more easily.

You Can Learn To Become Resilient

In order to become resilient, you must want it badly enough. Now, I realize this sounds silly, but it's not. If you live your life doing the same things day in and day out, you'll always get the same results. Perhaps this is working for you. If not, you must leave your safety net behind you. Jump out of your comfort zone and try something new. Granted, you may fail. And, it's okay if you fail. It's even great if you fail, sometimes. Otherwise, how will you learn to become resilient and bounce back after you've been punched down? These are called lessons in life and they help to develop resiliency and character.

Directed Journaling

❖ *Do you consider yourself to be an optimist or a pessimist? How do you know where you are on the scale? Is your glass half full or half empty? Why do you feel this way?*

❖ *What do you think formed your personality regarding optimism versus pessimism? Do you believe your parents played a huge role in your development or was it internal forces only? Describe in detail.*

❖ *Do you believe the research that optimistic people live longer, healthier, and happier lives? Why or why not?*

❖ *Do you, would you, go out on a limb and try new things? Is your personality a hardy one and if so, how do you know this? When did you first recognize this about yourself?*

❖ *Resiliency is important, yet, not everyone has this in their character. When you've been knocked down and sucker punched, have you been able to bounce back? How did you do it? Explain in detail. If you weren't able to bounce back before, do you think you could possibly do it now after reading this book?*

Look at Me Now—*You* Can Live Your Best Life Too, and Kick the Sucker Punched Crap to the Curb for Life!

"I've been knocked down so often as a little kid I can't count them. One might think those punches would end when I grew up and entered adulthood, but that was not the case. On a continual basis, I was sucker punched repeatedly during my thirties and forties. I didn't realize how strong I was until I began telling my stories to others. Helping people is and always has been my passion in life. I've dedicated myself to teaching individuals how to live free of fear. It sustains me and is my benchmark in helping others find their happiness."

~ Dr. Gayle Joplin Hall.

From Hell to H-e-l-l-o

Here we are in the final chapter of this book. You've read the stories I've told and somehow related them with things that've happened in your life, or the reverse. Perhaps none of the stories from the chapters in this book were like the life you've lived. But, what about the lives of your children, parents, or friends? Does any of this resonate with you? Have you ever been sucker punched? Do you know anyone who's been knocked down in life?

I went through hell and back for a reason. One of those reasons was to teach me patience, courage, and to help form my character as a strong, wise woman. There were many motives involved along the journey. I was forced to undergo unbearable bullying as a child so I could become the advocate and underdog for children and teens. I had to endure and suffer as a battered woman so that I could become the voice for victims of domestic violence. Getting pounded, knocked down, and sucker punched was hell. No, it was pure living hell. I went through hell in order to help you open doors, climb out of your shell, and say, "Hello world, it's my turn. It's my turn to live a beautiful life." Here we go!

Panties On the Line

Okay, I've shared most of my trash with you in this book. I must say it's pretty humbling and humiliating to discuss the sting of being bullied, of broken marriages, being cheated on, multiple relationships, being attacked by my ex-husband on hundreds of occasions, losing my job, going through midlife, suffering a nervous breakdown, and being duped by a family member. I've hung my panties out to dry and fully disclosed embarrassing, awkward, and upsetting times in my life so that

I may help you understand most of us have crap in our lives we must deal with. Every time I was sucker punched, it hurt. That pain and agony hurt my heart and it wounded my soul.

Sock It To Me

Everything changed when I learned that I had control over many things in my life. I didn't have to be the punching bag, stepping stool, or dirty clothes container when others wanted to get rid of their trash. I stopped living a life of fear—being afraid of people who might hurt me, being afraid of losing jobs, losing friends, losing money, losing respect, and just losing— it was ruining my life. Once I finally got the courage to stand up for myself and realized that I didn't have to put up with crap from anyone, and I do mean anyone, my entire life did a complete hundred and eighty degree turn. Nevertheless, I still needed the big guy to finalize what I had no control over. He was and is my boss in life.

God Steers My Car—Who Steers Yours?

I was literally in my Zen mode one night with my candles lit, sitting on the floor in my special place, chanting and rubbing warm stones, when I knew a big change was coming over me. The aroma from the candles filled the room with the scent of "Frosted Vanilla Cake." Completely relaxed, I asked for guidance from God. Now, for some reading this book, this may sound bogus. But for me, this is what I do when I am searching or when I feel lost. I turn to God and ask Him for direction.

God spoke to me in a magical way and led me to understand that He put me here on this Earth for a purpose. He told me to stop my constant searching as I tried to please everyone else. He guided me through grace to the place I am in my life right now.

I was instructed to avoid negativity at all costs, see the beauty in others if possible, and to spend time with those who appreciated my special talents. The voice I heard was distinct and the path was defined. He led me out of the darkness and into my life of really helping on a grand scale—one of earning my PhD, becoming a Lifestyle Coach, an International Best Selling Author, and an Empowerment Keynote Speaker. I loved teaching my students, but God called me to do more, to lead more using multiple platforms, and to teach more people how to face their fears and tackle being sucker punched, and help individuals become happy with their lives. I now have control over my life, but God will always sit in the driver's seat and be my boss.

Crawl If You Have To, Baby

You may be asking, "How do I start to get rid of the trash in my life? How do I avoid negative people? I am afraid I might piss somebody off. What should I do and how do I even begin to be happy?"

First, take a good look at your family. Do you feel safe and happy when you're home with your immediate family members? What about when you're with your extended family members? How do you feel then? If you're married, dating, or have blended or step-families, how do you feel when there's a family gathering, such as during the holidays? Is this a stressful time for you?

I will disclose that in my own family, I let one individual run races around me for almost two decades. This person told me when I could visit so I could be worked into the schedule. The funny thing is that I wanted to continue my relationship so badly that I did everything just as it was asked of me. I kept secrets. I always flew out of state, spent a lot of money and time to make the visits ensue, and worked hard to keep the relation-ship going. Not once in nineteen years had this person ever vis-ited me in my home. After breaking her/his word to me about coming to see me in my own home for a life-changing celebra-tion in my life, I realized that this family member did not value me. I drew the line and stated that I would see her/him again when the visit would be made to my home. This was not easy to do. However, each and every time I saw this family member, I would leave broken hearted because the utter coldness went through me like a razor-sharp knife. Each and every time, I was sucker punched in one way or another. It never felt good and cut my heart to the core.

Many individuals try to act like everyone's happy to see ev-erybody else when, in fact, some of the family members make each one in the group miserable. I've listened to story after story about how stressful the holidays are for families because there are so many expectations from family members regarding their relationships and the ability to get along. If you've worked for years to try to "like" someone and it hasn't worked because it's been one-sided on your part, give it up. This is more than likely completely different guidance than you've received before and may actually shock you. Dysfunctional families are infinite, but the great news is that you don't have to play. Walk away from the drama and if you can't walk away, crawl if you must. Just do yourself a favor and get out of there as quick as you can.

Confront the Demons

Research shows there are different ways of coping with stress, depending on your personality type and other factors. Psycho-therapy, self-help groups, and just disclosing with a trusted friend are some of the ways to cope and talk about problems that may be haunting you. Over a century ago, Freud recognized that catharsis was a way of disclosure through free association. This coping method also brought closure for many individuals. Cognitively, talking may also help you gain better insight overall.

True Loves Never Leave For Long

Men, women, boys, girls, neighbors, families, spouses, coworkers, students, associates, and clients all fall into one category when we're speaking of true loves. A true love is someone who never really leaves you. True loves stay in your heart wherever they may be and anywhere they go. They might live right next door to you or half-way across the world. What makes their relationship unique is love. The power of love conquers all, unlike any war or battle of words. When a person truly loves you unconditionally he or she looks past your flaws and uncovers the good in you. This same true love will be there by your side, even if it's only in spirit, to lift you up when you're having a crappy day or when you're lying in the hospital on your deathbed.

My best friend lives eleven hours away from me, yet I only get to see her about once every other year. When we meet, it's like we just saw each other yesterday. I've known her for over nineteen years. She knows all of my flaws and heard all of my heartaches and horror stories, yet she remains true to me. This person exhibits true love. She loves me unconditionally for the person I am and finds me to be a caring and beautiful woman. I am closer to her than I am with some of my own family members. Why? Because she cares about me and my life, and I genuinely care about her and the life she leads. We just have a very special connection.

Find a true love, or many. You only receive from a relationship what you're willing to put into the relationship. If you don't make time for this special person, you may lose him or her. Don't build walls around your heart. Otherwise, you'll keep true loves at a distance and miss out on all that is stunning and just waiting for you. True loves will contribute to your happiness.

Happiness is Not Found in a Bottle

It never ceases to amaze me how many people think that money will buy them happiness. We've all heard of people who've won the lottery and millions of dollars, only to be broke and miserable within the next two years. Why is this so? Perhaps it could be bad budgeting, but I highly doubt it. Studies have proven that wealthy people are not any happier than those with modest incomes. Money may buy you the opportunity of giving back to society or giving to others and living a more affluent lifestyle, but it will not make you happy.

Happiness is a choice and a decision, like a subjective well-being. People who are happy have high self-esteem, a sense of personal control, and are optimistic about their future. Research has shown that people are most happy on Fridays and Saturdays and least happy on Mondays and Tuesdays. Students are crabby in the mornings and happy in the early evenings. The three key predictors of happiness are 1) Social relationships, 2) Good physical health, and 3) Employment status—regardless of income. To me, this all makes sense.

If anyone had told me that I would be as happy as I am today, living my dream life like I am, when I was six years old, or twelve, or even twenty or thirty, I wouldn't have believed it. I love my life now and you can love your life, too.

Live Your Best Life Now!

In this final chapter, we've discussed taking control of your life so that you can learn to live free from fear. Be bold and remove yourself from unhealthy relationships or situations that do nothing but cause you angst. Take control, jump into the driver's seat if you must, and bust free from the stress that's holding you back. Name it, claim it, own it—all the garbage. Bag it up and drag it all out to the dumpster.

Realize who you can trust and then talk about your issues. When you think you're finished talking, then talk some more. Perhaps you need to visit with a lifestyle coach, a psychotherapist, your family doctor, or your very best friend. Maybe your closest ally is a family member. Just be sure to disclose everything that is bothering you so you can release this toxic waste from your body. Get rid of all of it. Do this now. Then, get your booty ready for what is about to happen next.

Find your true love(s) or rebuild your relationships with those you cherish now that you have more time since the garbage is not leaving a stench in your house. This is paramount for your happiness. Love yourself first and then love like you've never loved before. You deserve this.

You can live your best life now if you read this entire book, execute the directed journaling at the end of each chapter, and have the will to want to live your best life now. Some people say they want to live a life that is glorious, but they won't take the steps it takes to get rid of the stink first. I ask that you follow the steps in this book so that you won't be a target for being sucker punched on a regular basis. You already have everything you need inside you to create a new self-fulfilling prophecy and live the life you deserve if you're willing to allow it. We only get one shot at this thing called life, so make it your best.

Directed Journaling

❖ Have you ever felt like you've been to hell and back, like being sucker punched? Describe the situation. How did you handle it? If you haven't experienced this yourself, tell the story of one of your family members, co-workers, or friends. How was the problem solved?

❖ If you need to "take out the garbage" like I described in this chapter, how would you do it? I mean, explain exactly how you are going to rid yourself of the trash.

❖ When you disclose or tell your story, who listens to you? Are they attentive? Do you feel better after you have talked out loud about your issues? If you have answered "no" to any of these questions, you need to find a new best friend—fast.

❖ What do you feel like you have control over in your life? How does this make you feel? Do you understand that there are some things we can never have control over (such as other people's words or actions), so we must remove ourselves from them if they become caustic to us?

❖ Please envision living your best life now. What do you see when you first wake up? Where do you live? What do you smell? What will fill your time today? If someone tries to spoil your day with a sneak sucker punch, how will you handle that? Will you let this derail you, now that you have read this book? If so, start at the beginning and read Sucker Punched™ again. Be sure to work through the directed journaling at the end of every chapter.

Dr. Hall's next book is: *Sucker Punched!™ in Love*. You won't want to miss it. It will include stories told by others who have been punched down in relationships and love. Perhaps your story will be fitting for this book. Contact Dr. Hall if you'd like the opportunity to contribute to her next book, *Sucker Punched!™ in Love*.

About the Author

Gayle Joplin Hall, PhD: Doctor in Psychology, is a Lifestyle Health and Relationship Coach; best-selling, three-time published author; keynote empowerment speaker; and expert in domestic violence, crisis analysis, and behavior consultation. She is a professor and Mentor. Dr. Hall is President, CEO, and Founder of Dr. G. J. Hall Enterprises, LLC. Dr. Hall on Call™ is based on the philosophy of positive psychology and the law of attraction.

Gayle has studied human behavior for over two decades. What she's noticed is a common factor among people everywhere— we have choices to be happy with our lives or to make changes. Many people remain stuck in their situations because of fear. As a victor of Domestic Violence, Gayle realized this about herself. Fear of failure had kept her from pursuing her dreams of fulfilling her mission to reach global audiences with multiple platforms. This included starting her coaching business, speaking engagements, co-authoring books, and writing her own first two books. The first book is titled, *Sucker Punched!*™. She is now transparent and shares her stories, life, and wisdom with the world.

"It makes me a better person to be a part of something bigger." As one of the touchstone quotes in Gayle's repertoire, this has grounded her for over twenty years. Gayle has donated over five thousand hours of service to victims of domestic violence. She has served thirty-two families with hospice during their times of need. Her service work encompasses the homeless population, the isolated elderly, Veterans and the USO, homeless children and the YWCA, and BACA.

Caring, compassion, dedication, happiness, integrity, laughing, loving, and serving—these words encompass Gayle Joplin Hall's core belief system. Gayle will guide you in decisions about love, relationships, careers, goal-setting, anxiety, dating, divorce, meditation, fear, PTSD, conflict resolution, children, happiness, LGBT, stress, spirituality, and more. The value she brings to each person's life resonates long after her work is finished.

Dr. Gayle Hall's many professional speaking engagements include audiences as small as groups of five to groups of fifteen hundred people. Contact Gayle for help in discovering your bliss and passion. To schedule your "Hall-Call" or to book a speaking engagement, please visit: www.DrHallonCall.com. Gayle's private email is: gaylehallphd@gmail.com.

For more information about the author,
Dr. Gayle Joplin Hall, please visit her website:
www.DrHallonCall.com.

Be sure to sign up on the email list and become
part of our community.

We are growing and do not want to leave you behind.

Godspeed, Be Happy, and Live Your Best Life Now!

Dr. Gayle Joplin Hall